HOLOCAUST EDUCATION

A RESOURCE BOOK FOR TEACHERS AND PROFESSIONAL LEADERS

edited

by

Marcia Sachs Littell

Symposium Series
Volume 13

The Edwin Mellen Press
New York and Toronto

A Report of the Eighth Annual Philadelphia Conference
on Teaching the Holocaust
24-26 October 1982

Holocaust Education: A Resource Book For Teachers
And Professional Leaders
Edited by Marcia Sachs Littell

Symposium Series   Volume 13
Series ISBN 0-88946-989-X

Published by The Edwin Mellen Press
in cooperation with
The Anne Frank Institute of Philadelphia

For Information contact:
The Edwin Mellen Press
P.O. Box 450
Lewiston, New York 14092

Printed in the United States of America

This volume on liberty and
persecution is dedicated
to the Russian branch of
the family I have never
known --

My maternal grandparents,
  Manya and Yitzack
My mother's sister,
  Seepa

and to my cousins living
still in Kiev - Eva, Rose,
Manya and Beba.

                    M. S. L.

Dick Thornburgh is Governor of the Commonwealth of Pennsylvania.

Franklin H. Littell is Founder and Honorary Chairman of the National Institute on the Holocaust and a professor at Temple University.

Yehuda Bauer is a professor at Hebrew University and a founder of the Center for the Scientific Study of Antisemitism.

Hubert G. Locke is co-founder of the Annual Scholars Conference on the Church Struggle and the Holocaust and a professor at the University of Washington.

A. Leon Higginbotham, Jr. is Judge in the U.S. Circuit Court of Appeals for the Third District.

Robert W. Ross is a professor at the University of Minnesota.

J. Willard O'Brien is Dean of the Law School at Villanova University.

A. H. Raskin is Associate Director of the National News Council.

Alton I. Sutnick is Dean of the Medical College of Pennsylvania.

Roger Winter is Director of the U.S. Committee for Refugees.

Deborah Hertz is a professor at the State University of New York: Binghamton.

Richard L. Rubenstein is Professor of Religious Studies at Florida State University.

Theodore R. Mann is Chairman of the National Conference on Soviet Jewry and a partner in Mann and Unger law firm in Philadelphia.

Michael Feuer teaches at Drexel University and is former President of the Philadelphia Sons and Daughters of Holocaust Survivors.

Mel Mermelstein is a survivor and businessman, founder of the Auschwitz Study Foundation.

CONTENTS

FOREWORD

These proceedings include the major presentations of the Eighth Annual Teaching Conference. The theme of the Eighth Conference on Teaching the Holocaust and Its Lessons was "Lessons of the Holocaust: Signs of Oppression."

The major working groups concentrated on the teaching task, with special attention to two public sectors. First, the needs of teachers in the schools, on campuses, and in the congregations were a major focus. Second, the challenge to the professions was a major focus. In the Third Reich, the several professions debased themselves and besmirched basic standards of professional ethics and morality. The record of the Holocaust raises serious questions requiring self-examination by professional persons and groups in the post-Auschwitz world.

With the twentieth century often referred to as the age of genocide, the overall task of the Eighth Teaching Conference was to ascertain, first, if after nearly four decades the lessons of the Holocaust have taught us to identify those factors that contribute to the liberty, dignity and integrity of the human person. Second, what lessons have been learned about the important responsibility of each citizen in a democracy. Are we now able to identify oppressive signs when they are in our midst? Has the Holocaust taught us that liberty is not a cotton candy affair - that we must respect it, that we must protect it? Societies that do not defend and expand areas of liberty do not remain static: they go bad, sliding from bigotry to persecution to genocide.

The papers presented at the Eighth Annual Teaching Conference highlight those areas in which we have progressed and those areas in which more work is required. We move forward in our work always mindful of Elie Wiesel's words regarding the Holocaust: "...a uniquely Jewish tragedy with universal implications."

Marcia Sachs Littell

INTRODUCTION

According to the Jewish and Christian Scriptures, after an epoch-making event the people must spend "forty years in the wilderness" before they begin to comprehend what has happened to them. During these forty years a few seers and prophets and teachers meditate and mull over the event. And then, with distance, there comes a rush of interpretation. The fire that only a few daring spirits once approached is now surrounded by throngs. The danger of commercialization and vulgarization becomes acute, and the poets and prophets and teachers are hard pressed that the central message may be transmitted uncorrupted to children and children's children.

Like the Exodus from Egypt, the Holocaust is an event of that mass - in the history of a particular people, and also in the history of many tribes and families and peoples.

Today we speak of the meaning and also of the lessons of the Holocaust. And we teach these things, lest the terrible losses of that dark night of iniquity be counted vain.

Of the practical lessons, none is more important than the development of an Early Warning System to identify potentially genocidal movements. The German Nazi Party was a terrorist movement, potentially genocidal, for more than a decade before it took power. What are the signs today by which like movements can be identified and subdued with a minimum of violence? What are the lessons to be learned, that red flags and ringing bells may go up in the educated minds when the parameters of civility and reasonable dissent and loyal opposition have been transgressed in the public forum?

Our 1982 Philadelphia Conference on Teaching the Holocaust was aimed at opening up the lessons of the Holocaust, at pointing toward an identification "grid" to spare generations to come the tragedy that comes when evil is let to run unchecked and when evil men are let loose upon the commonwealth.

Franklin H. Littell

RENEWING OUR COMMITMENT

GOVERNOR DICK THORNBURGH

When I first took office as Governor of this state, I did not foresee that some day, Ginny and I, during a visit to Israel, would have the somber experience of visiting the memorial to the Holocaust victims at Yad Vashem.

I didn't expect that our travel plans would include a trip to the Soviet Union, where we would see first-hand the oppression of people whose only crime was to be Jewish.

It has been our good fortune in the past three-and-a-half years to become deeply and personally involved with the hopes, the concerns and the dreams of Jewish people around the world.

In short, our awareness of the Jewish experience, and what it means to the freedom of all people, everywhere, has been enhanced in ways we will treasure forever.

One would have to have a heart of stone not to be impressed by the woman I met in the Soviet Union whose quiet strength and towering character transcended any language barriers, a woman who has felt the joy and endured the pain of being the mother of Anatoly Shcharansky.

My meeting with Ida Migrom, this remarkable woman, came at the close of an eight-day tour of the Soviet Union in 1979, a tour by several American governors that confirmed much of what we had heard about the oppressive climate in which Soviet Jews must live, and love, and struggle for the right to maintain the culture of their forebears in the training and education of their children.

If there is anything that particularly remains in my memory of that trip, it was the anti-Semitism that not only seems to permeate life in Soviet society, but also comes close to serving as an instrument of government policy, an attitude made clear to us in subtle, yet repeated remarks of Soviet bureaucrats.

It was made clear to us in the not-so-subtle proliferation of books stamped "only for official use" in that country—books with titles like "Facism Under the Blue Star" and "Zionism in the System of Anti-Sovietism."

It was made clear to us in the prohibition of the teaching of the Hebrew language to new generations, a prohibition akin to cultural genocide.

And it was made tragically clear to us at the World War II

memorial at Minsk--where our government guides conveniently forgot
to note that the Jewish population of that city had been reduced
from roughly half the pre-war total population, to only five percent
today.

We saw these things, heard these things, and knew these things.

But when we met the mother of Shcharansky, we knew that defeat
and despair aren't necessarily the same. In three years, Ida Milgrom
had been unable to obtain defense counsel in her own country for her
son. As a founder of the legal services program here in Pennsylvania,
I found myself wanting to file an appeal, only to realize I was in a
land in which that very concept is an alien one.

But Mrs. Milgrom was not defeated. She asked us to thank all
Americans who had raised a voice of protest from the very day of
her son's arrest. She said the outcry from here and elsewhere had
literally saved her son's life, and she asked that we not forget the
larger fight for freedom, a fight of which he is but a part.

To this day, Anatoly Shcharansky remains in prison. News reports say he began a hunger strike at the end of September to protest repeated confiscation of his mail. Mrs. Milgrom fears her son
could die from it since he is still weak from six months of solitary
confinement last year.

I know all of you join me in praying that Shcharansky will survive this latest difficulty in a brave life fraught with hardship,
and that someday, he will find the freedom that has been denied him.

What Mrs. Milgrom, her son, and other dissidents I met in the
Soviet Union ask is that we not lapse into apathy--that although we
are on the other side of the world, we hold the bright flame of their
struggle aloft, rather than buried under the weight of our own day-to-
day concerns.

I contend that we must do the same to keep the memory of the
Holocaust alive.

One way of dealing with the unspeakable atrocities committed
during that period of infamy would be to put them out of our minds--
to leave them behind as quickly and completely as possible, as one
tends to do with painful and tragic memories.

Instead, Jews and other concerned citizens such as are gathered
here today, have chosen to examine the Holocaust--to examine it as
dispassionately as possible, for only in that fashion can we truly
uncover the roots of that almost unbelievable era.

In doing so, you are indeed performing a public service for all
victims of inhumanity, regardless of color, religion, or background,

and regardless of the nature of their oppressors.

At this point of the conference, you must have heard at least a dozen times that the lessons of the Holocaust must not be forgotten—that ignorning them would be tantamount to promoting the very things that led to the Holocaust in the first place.

Yet, it is terribly important to recognize that to allow the implications of the Holocaust to fade into distant memory would be to hasten that day when humanity might once again suspend the decency without which this would be a monstrous world.

It's heartening, indeed essential, therefore, to see people of diverse religions and ethnic backgrounds working together to make sure that the horror of the past shall not fade from our consciousness.

I am especially pleased by the efforts of Philadelphians in this regard.

It was in this city that the first Conference on the Holocaust was held, in 1975. That, and succeeding Holocaust conferences helped spawn others across the contry, and introduced certain initiatives such as teaching about the Holocaust in public schools.

It was in this city that the first monument to the Holocaust on American public property was erected—at 16th Street and the Parkway.

I am proud, too, that Pennsylvanians consistently have worked to affirm the Jewish spirit and our ties with Israel. I note, particularly, that the "Liberty Garden" in the center of Jerusalem, which I was able to visit in 1980, has been heavily supported by Pennsylvanians and contains a replica of the same Liberty Bell we revere near Independence Hall.

Whether these types of initiatives are symbolic, or more direct in approach, they strengthen ties among Jews, and between all people. They help us assure that those gruesome forces that often succeed in alienating person from person, neighbor from neighbor, nation from nation, and those of one religion, race or culture from another, will never prevail over decency and humanity—not here, in Pennsylvania, not here in America, and not in any other nation on this earth.

The lesson that those of us in public office can learn from all of this is that we must constantly renew our commitment that the Holocaust remain a thing of the past that must never be repeated—and constantly renew our commitment to the pursuit of human rights, human compassion, and human understanding among all people, in all places, for all time.

THE FUTURE OF HOLOCAUST EDUCATION

DR. FRANKLIN H. LITTELL

A dozen years ago, when the first academic conference was held to deal with the Holocaust and related matters (Detroit, 1970), little was being done to teach the Holocaust and its lessons. And nothing was heard in reputable circles to deny the facts of the event. Today, we find ourselves in a totally different situation, one rich in promise --but fraught with danger and conflict.

To deal with the negative side first, the denial of the event is now bobbing to the surface in campus circles. Within the last six months, we have encountered listings of books by "revisionist historians" at Los Angeles Community College, the University of Miami and Kutztown State College--among others. Whereas a citizen of courage, like Mel Mermelstein (who is present among us), has pursued and defeated the deniers in their lair, the academic communities have as yet shown no such concern or self-respect. In this, too, we are seeing in the American colleges and universities the same moral flabbiness that made it possible for German Nazis to infiltrate and demoralize the universities of the Weimar Republic.

When systemwide attention to the Holocaust began in our high schools, Colonel Walter J. Fellenz, who was three decades before the commander of the combat infantry troops that opened Dachau, commented as follows:

"To me, the Holocaust was one of the most shameful crimes since man walked the earth. More shameful, however, is the fact that the forces of evil are trying to deny that this Holocaust ever took place."(1

Colonel Fellenz praised the teaching of the Holocaust. Like those who attended the International Liberators' Conference in Washington, D.C. last fall, and those who attended the International Survivors" Conference in Tel-Aviv in the Spring of 1981, he was convinced of the importance of the event in human history--and of the importance of resolutely confronting those who would deny the facts.

The mission of the so-called revisionist historians has nothing to do with historical scholarship, of course, and none of their masthead group on the well-financed Journal of Historical Revision qualifies as a professional historian. Their mission is political, and it must be confronted with statesmanship--in public, on the campuses, and in the schools.

Telling the Story

When we turn to the positive side, the teaching of the Holocaust and its lessons, the picture is much more encouraging--on the campuses, in the junior and senior high schools, and in the congregations. Whereas in 1970 there were no more than a dozen courses in colleges and universities, a survey made two years ago by Prof. Byron Sherwin of Spertus College (co-editor of one of the best books in the Field: Encountering the Holocaust: An Interdisciplinary Approach, 1979) registered over 800 courses in the Holocaust on American campuses. At Temple University, where we set up the first Ph.D. in Holocaust Studies in cooperation with the program at the Institute of Contemporary Jewry, Hebrew University, we have just graduated our first student--an Israeli, Mordecai Paldiel, who defended his dissertation "with distinction." The Annual Scholars Conference still functions every Spring for professors and graduate students, now meeting in New York and sponsored by the National Conference of Christians and Jews.

At high school level, we are justifiably proud of the fact that the first system-wide instruction was inaugurated in Philadelphia in 1975-76. To be sure, the first single program of instruction had been launched at Great Barrington, Massachusetts in 1972. With the assistance and counsel of Dr. Bernhard Olsen of the National Conference of Christians and Jews, whose study Faith and Prejudice (1961) is still the best work in the field, two teachers at Great Barrington developed an important voluntary course. But in 1975, under the initiative and leadership of Dr. Ezra Staples, Dr. George French, Jr., and Mr. Harold Kessler, the Philadelphia high schools moved forward in a pace-setting way. A year and a half later, New York followed suit. More recently, the parochial high schools of the Archdiocese of Philadelphia--largely thanks to the statesmanship of Sister Gloria Coleman--became the first Roman Catholic system in the country to teach the Holocaust.

Now, at the National Institute on the Holocaust we hear every week from some high school or regional board that wants literature and professional help in launching the teaching of the Holocaust. Just this month, we participated in the planning and carrying out of the first Holocaust conference in the state of Maine. Held at Bates College, the conference there was initiated by Gerda Haas (a survivor, author of a splendid book: These I Do Remember, 1982) and drew teachers from all over the state.

The international dimension is especially important. We have always stressed that the teaching of the Holocaust and its lessons must be interfaith, interdisciplinary and international. The first conference on the Holocaust on German soil grew out of the core group of the Annual Scholars Conference, and the first university seminar on the Holocaust in the Bundesrepublik was taught at Marburg by Dr. Erich Geldbach--a participant in the 1978 Philadelphia Conference, presently an adjunct member of the board of the National Institute. The Annual Teachers Institute at Yad Vashem in Jerusalem, at which the Director and Honorary Chairman of the National Institute regularly lecture, has asked the National Institute to serve as the recruitment and screening office for teachers coming to Yad Vashem from the United States.

Nor should we forget the congregations, Jewish and Christian, when we survey the astonishing expansion of Holocaust education in the last decade. Year by year, the number of Jewish congregations observing Yom haShoah has increased. In 1973, there were seven Christian congregations holding special services in memory of the 6,000,000; last year, there were hundreds. In fact, under the aegis of the U. S. Holocaust Memorial Council, Yom haShoah has become a public observance. Last year, proclamations were issued by the President, joined by 44 governors and dozens of mayors of cities. The number of congregations teaching the Holocaust cannot be counted, but it is certain that in Holocaust education, the hymns, psalms, prayers and liturgies of the congregations reach more numbers and more fundamentally than all of the learned books and articles of the academics.

Something very important has happened in Holocaust education, and in the public awareness of the importance of the telling of the story. Ten years ago, a diligent scholar could know most of the writers and most of the bibliography; today, it is scarcely possible to keep up with the articles and books that appear every month. What has happened is that we have passed through the Scriptural "forty years in the wilderness," and the uncertainty and the numbness has passed. A new literary genre has appeared: the narratives of survivors, the poems and plays and music and art forms of interpreters, the essays of the critics. Even the scholarly articles and books are now too numerous, and the flood swells weekly, for any single individual to keep abreast of developments.

The foolish ask, "Why trouble us 40 years after the incident?" The wise know that we have just begun to explore the sheer mass of the event, with all of its meaning(s). A few years ago, Nelly Sachs, who shared the Nobel Prize for Literature in 1966, and Elie Wiesel, whose book Night has had an influence comparable to The Diary of Anne Frank, were working as solitaries. Today, a whole generation of artists and writers is coming to public attention and demanding of us that we listen and respond to the story of the Holocaust. We are fortunate in having the tactile, the optical presentations, for no essay and no speech can equal in impact the displays at Yad Vashem, Lohamei haGhettaot, Bet Hatfusoth. For this reason, the Anne Frank Center, recently projected for Philadelphia, is so important. There are 15 or 16 Anne Frank centers in Western Europe, a dozen in Israel, but—again—Philadelphia has a "first": the first Anne Frank Center in the Americas has been announced, and will be opened, in Philadelphia in the next few months. Here pupils will see as well as hear the story of Anne Frank, of "Tolka"—leader of resistance to the Nazis in the Vilna area, of survivors who have made a new life in the new world. A generation that desperately needs models will meet models in the heroes and heroines of the Holocaust.

Teaching the Lessons of the Holocaust

When we turn to the matter of teaching the lessons of the Holocaust, to which our annual conferences on teaching the Holocaust have increasingly turned, we run into special difficulties.

Who has the right to speak? only survivors? Who dares to treat with scientific objectivity the "data" of such an event, awash in a flood of tears?

Nevertheless, the demand is placed upon us every day: "What can be learned that will prevent a repetition of such agony and suffering?" The survivors require it. The liberators demand it. Parents, asking what may be taught the children, lay upon us a burden that cannot be lightly discharged. Those of us who are called to teach cannot turn aside from the task, however difficult we may personally find it.

First, under the insistent demand that such a thing must not happen again, we have come to see the importance of developing an Early Warning System. How do we identify and single out, and render impotent, movements that are potentially genocidal? After all, it is the element of predictability that makes a science. We do not have a science when an observer, however careful, describes a cholera epidemic. We have a science when there is a group of experts who can tell us, in time, that given certain conditions we are going to have a cholera epidemic.

In an Early Warning System, what are the elements which we can discern as danger signals? When are there enough such characteristics to send a warning signal? Certainly one of the lessons of the Holocaust is this: We must identify and neutralize such factors and forces before they become strong enough to induce civil war, or--God forbid-- seize power and murder their opponents.

Second, and following on this initial point, we understand that one of the central lessons of the Holocaust is this: The German Nazi Party was a terrorist movement before it became a criminal government with the power to commit genocide. A number of conferences have been held recently to study terrorism in the shadow of Auschwitz. In Orlando, Florida, a fine conference on Holocaust studies was followed a year later by a conference on terrorism; the first drew teachers from all over the northern part of the state; the second drew law enforcement officials from cities, counties and state agencies. There is a rising realization that although the USA has been spared the attacks and de- stabilizing tactics of terrorist bands that have undermined self- government and liberty in France, West Germany, England and the Nether- lands--and virtually destroyed them in Italy, the time is approaching when the disorder and violence for which the Weathermen, Socialist Workers Party, KuKlux Klan and American Nazis are striving so dili- gently will put the republic to the test.

Third: We understand that the Holocaust confronts the modern

university with a credibility crisis. The massive crime of the Holocaust
was committed by professors and Ph.Ds—not to forget the M.D.s. Robert
J. Lifton, who has been with us in previous conferences, has a splendid
study of "Medicalized Killing in Auschwitz," based upon interviews and
study of over 90 S.S. doctors. His work continues with new evidence and
insights the questions opened up by Max Weinrich in his great volume,
Hitler's Professors—published in 1946, and one of the miracles of
prescience in this area.

It is clear that the universities and professional schools have not
yet faced the implications of the fact that Dr. Freisler and Dr. Mengele
were trained by great universities—the German universities before the
Nazis corrupted them. The recent reports from the Medical School and
the Law School of Harvard University, for example, both indicate no
awareness of the moral and ethical questions put by the Holocaust. On
the other hand, there are exceptions: the recent Institute established
by Professor Willard O'Brien of the Villanova Law School, to deal with
questions of religion, ethics and law, is a very encouraging and important potential. According to Professor O'Brien, it was his experience in this series of annual teaching conferences that moved him to
found the Institute and to leave the post of Dean of the Law School
to give full time to the Institute. Like many of us, he has found that
this side of the Holocaust nothing is ever the same again.

In point of fact, study of the Holocaust is in many respects not
unlike pathological studies in a medical school. Careful study of
corrupt bodies may give one clues as to the meaning of health. Analog-
ically, careful study of the Holocaust—and of society under the Third
Reich—can be meaningful to all branches of humane learning. A strong
case can be made that Sociology, Political Science, Psychology, Literature, Religion, Anthropology, Social Psychology, Education, Criminal
Justice, Biology, Journalism, et al., are greatly illuminated when
attention is paid to their pathological as well as positive materials.
In sum, not only the professional schools but university instruction
in general will be greatly improved as the lessons of the Holocaust
penetrate the always conservative centers of Academe.

Fourth: We understand that a basic lesson of the Holocaust is the
need to correct certain long-standing Christian preachings and teachings
about the Jewish people. Although Nazi antisemitism had pagan as well
as Christian components, there is no question but that centuries of
Christian antisemitism created a situation within which modern political/
ideological antisemitism could flourish. With German and Dutch colleagues,
with American theologians like Paul van Buren, Roy Eckardt, John Pawlikow-
ski and Leonard Swindler, with the collegial cooperation of Jewish teachers
like Emil Fackenheim and Irving Greenberg, we are making clear progress in
transmuting prejudice and error into fraternity and truth.

The most striking achievement of any church judicatory to date is
that of the Rheinland Synod, which in January, 1980, issued a statement

on the Jewish people that has not been equalled elsewhere as yet. The
Rheinland church is the wealthiest, and probably the largest, Protestant
church in Europe. The statement upon which their synod agreed over-
whelmingly stated, among other things:

> "recognition of Christian co-responsibility and guilt for
> the Holocaust...
> "new biblical insights concerning the continuing significance
> of the Jewish people for salvation history...
> "the insight that the continuing existence of the Jewish
> people, its return to the Land of Promise, and also the
> creation of the State of Israel are signs of the faithfulness
> of God toward God's people..."(2

Fifth: We understand the importance of legitimate government, in
contrast to the totalitarian government under which neither human liberty/
dignity/integrity nor popular sovereignty can grow. And we know how
rare governments that are representative, and have a record of respect
to civil liberties, are on the world map. A few months ago, a survey
of the governments represented in the United Nations Assembly showed
this breakdown:

Marxist dictatorships	26
Muslim dictatorships	17
military dictatorships (junta-type)	28
old-fashioned despotisms	14
republics, new and precariously situated	30
constitutional monarchies, with a record of toleration	9
republics, stable but with established religion	12
republics, stable and with religious liberty and representative government	13

Which is to say that 115 of the governments represented in the UN Assembly
are going to be wrong on every issue pertaining to human dignity and
human rights, before any discussion is held or vote taken. This clari-
fied for me, among other things, what kind of people would cheer an
Arafat and an Idi Amim: Arafat and Idi Amim are their kind of people.

Sixth: We understand the importance of religious liberty. One of
the major lessons of the Holocaust is this: the close cooperation between church and state which obtained from the time of the Emperor
Constantine was a danger to Jews and a curse to Christian dissenters.
As Jules Isaac emphasized in his great work, Jesus and Israel (1959,
1971), the turning point in Christian antisemitism and repression and
the starting point of Christian triumphalism were one and the same.
At the time of the rise of Hitler, the landesherrliche Kirchenregiment
had so corrupted the Protestant churches, and the Concordat system had
so corrupted the Roman Catholic dioceses, that even had the church
leaders recognized and confronted the Evil One they were virtually

powerless to act. But they did not, except for small minorities, confront it: on July 20, 1933, Pacelli (later Pius XII) struck the deal
with Hitler that gave the Fuhrer his first great diplomatic victory
and made him salonfahig (fit for social intercourse).

Constitutional authorities assure us that the greatest contribution of the American system to the science of government is precisely
this: the separation of the political covenant from religious commitments. This means that government is to stay out of the religion
business, and that no religious clique or cabal is to manipulate
government. Government is "secular" and religion is voluntary. As
fellow-Americans, we are to forego the ancient practice, common for
a millenium and a half in Christendom, of using repression and coercion
and violence against those of other conscience and convictions. Yet,
accepting our present pluralism, we are to join hands in cooperation
with persons of conscience on all matters affecting the health and well-
being of the commonwealth.

Finally, with our awareness of the fragile nature of inter-religi-
ous amity and cooperation, with our awareness of how rare liberty and
self-government are on the world map, a basic lesson of the Holocaust
is the importance of our covenant of brotherhood. Abraham Lincoln
would not accept the opinions of those who intended to rend the republic
because he sensed that their proposals and intention were outside the
arena of good faith and proper debate. Today, we will not accept the
opinions of terrorists and extremists because we sense that they do
not intend the common good: their purpose is power, and the destruction of the republic and the liberties of loyal citizens. Today, as
we reflect on the meaning of the Holocaust, we are moved to pledge
again to each other the hand of brotherhood--of brotherhood that has,
in America at its best, bound in common destiny black and white and
brown, Christian and Jew.

The future of Holocaust education is secure because the ashes of
Auschwitz have been moulded with other elements into a mirror: in
that mirror we perceive what can happen when love and justice are forgotten and men become the servants of necrophiliac machines. The
story of the Holocaust will be told, and the lessons of the Holocaust
will be taught, long after you and I are gone. And day by day, we
see a change occurring in its impact; that which was once sheer agony
and trauma is being transmuted into lessons of hope and healing; that
which was once uniquely Jewish is, like the Exodus of old, the carrier
of truths of import to all families and tribes and nations that have
eyes to see and ears to hear.

NOTES:

1. Letter to the Editor, in THE NEW YORK TIMES, 12/22/77

2. Translated and published in XVII JOURNAL OF ECUMENICAL STUDIES (1980) 1:211-12

LESSONS OF THE HOLOCAUST: SIGNS OF OPPRESSION

Dr. Yehuda Bauer

Thank you Sister Gloria. I think that it is true to say that any
historical event undergoes transformations after it happens, in the consciousness of the people who know about it, studied it, and remember it.
The greater, the more important the event, the more true this is; the
event undergoes these transformations sometimes to the extent of a misuse or abuse of the original event. One might say that it is a situation
where a certain historical occurrence occurs really twice or at least
twice: once, when it actually happens; and then, when it is talked about,
written about, enters into what one might call the historical consciousness of a period. This is even more true regarding an event which I
believe to be one of the two decisive events of the 20th century, along
with the use of the atomic bomb in Hiroshima and Nagasaki. It is perhaps
no surprise that the event itself should then be distorted and changed and
put into categories into which it really doesn't belong at all, and it is
the specific task of historians and of others to try to cut through this
web of myths of misstatements, many of them unintentional and made in
good faith, and return as closely as one can back to what actually
happened. Now, when one talks about the lessons of the Holocaust, the
first lesson of the Holocaust is to know something about it. This
elementary truth is often forgotten in a stream of justified emotional
response, of justified concern with the aftermath, with the after-effects.
The knowledge, or at least a certain modicum of knowledge about the
Holocaust itself is a prerequisite for anything else that we might do.
In that context, I want to concentrate on just one point, and that is the
uniqueness of the Holocaust, and its universality. This, of course, is
something to which many of us have been devoting our time and energy and
writing capabilities for a long time. The uniqueness of the Holocaust
lay not in the number of the victims, and not even in the method of their
destruction, although the gas chambers were put up for Jews and had it not
been for the Jews, I doubt that this kind of machinery would have been
established; but in the gas chambers, along with millions of Jews,
thousands of Gypsies, thousands of Soviet prisoners of war and some others
also died. So, it isn't that. The uniqueness lies in the motivation of
the perpetrator. Who was the Jew in the eye of the Nazis? Why the
destruction? The destruction came because the Jew was viewed as a
Satanic element in human society. As an extra-human on earth. Walther
Buch, a party judge of the National Socialist Party, said in 1937, that
the Jew is not a human being; he is a symbol of decadence.
"Faulniserscheinung," in German. When you excluded the Jew from what
Helen Fine in her book ACCOUNTING FOR GENOCIDE called 'the universe of
human obligation,' when you saw the Jew as a non-human, then certain
logical consequences had to follow. The Jew was seen as the central
problem of humanity; this is so unbelievable that it is frightfully

difficult to teach this. Let me tell you that not only I or people like myself dealing with this, but German historians such as Karl D. Bracher or Andreas Hillgruber tell us today that Hitler went to war for two main reasons. Problems of strategy, or economics were incidentals. He went to war in order to establish Germanic supremacy in Europe and the world; and in order to achieve that, he aimed at the elimination of the 'Jewish world government,' supposedly ruling America, ruling Bolshevik Russia, ruling France, and trying to rule England. Germany rose in defense against this Jewish world threat. So, the last time anti-semitism took hold over a great society and a great nation, it was one of the two main causes of a war of six years and 35 million dead before it was over. That is a lesson of the Holocaust. Now, Simon Wiesenthal, a man who has earned the respect of all of us for his great work in hunting down Nazis, says that there were 11 million victims of the Holocaust--6 million Jews and 5 million non-Jews. This is sheer and utter nonsense. There were not 5 million non-Jews killed in the Second World War. You don't have to call something a Holocaust.if you want to work against it. The murder of millions of Russians, Poles, Frenchmen, Serfs and many others is a frightful crime in its own "right." It has to be fought; it has to be discussed; it has to be treated in its own right, in its own way. It is true that for the people who died there is no difference between Holocaust and other types of murder. Whether one was killed at Auschwitz or whether one was a Pole and was shot in the action of the Germans against the Polish intelligentia--one death is like any other death. But for the living, it makes a big difference because you must differentiate between evil and evil. Just as you would differentiate between good and good. Surely everyone knows the difference between helping an old lady across the street or saving that same lady from a burning building. We differentiate between good and good. We differentiate between a pickpocket and a murderer. You do it in any case, in any society. Any society with law courts, with a justice department, knows there is a difference between evil and evil. Equally, there is a difference between these ultimate ways of doing evil things. It won't do for this wonderful audience to go out into the streets of Philadelphia with banners saying-- "We are against evil." They'll laugh at you, and rightly so, because all evil is particular, though the lessons are universal. The Holocaust is a Jewish experience--and I am not in the game of 'my Holocaust is better than yours.' It's a Jewish experience because the motivation was anti-Jewish and that makes it a universal business because the background of Nazism is in European society, is in Christian thought and in Christian apostasy and in German pagan tradition. It is universal because it could happen to others, or to Jews, and I said here before at one of these conferences and I'll say it again: who knows who the Jews might be next time? If that is so, it is a universal lesson from a particular experience.

This discussion is taking place in that part of the world where free discussion is possible. But we are living in a world where democratic societies are not exactly on the increase, where a large part of the world is under all kinds of authoritarian and dictatorial regimes. Signs of oppression? Don't you see oppression all around the place? But when we talk about signs of oppression, we mean ourselves. We mean that

society where we can discuss these things, and that society is
vulnerable, it faces tremendous problems. When we talk about the
Holocaust, we have to get our terminology right. In the last hundred
years or so, we have been faced with destruction ranging from mass
murder through genocide to Holocaust. Genocide really means the
forcible denationalization of a people, with a more selective mass
murder of many of its members, as happened to the Polish people during
the Second World War, with its intelligentsia murdered, with sections
in the western part of the country of the Catholic clergy arrested
and many of them killed in Nazi concentration camps, with 3 million
Poles dying, with the intention of the Nazis to eliminate the Polish
nation as such, but not to murder all Poles. They did not intend to
murder all Poles because, among other things, they needed them as slaves.
That was Genocide. What is Holocaust? It is the planned total mass
annihilation of a people and the execution of that plan. That happened
once, to the Jew and something not dissimilar happened to the Armenians.
But once I've said that, I define Holocaust as a general form because
what happened to the Jews could happen in one form or another to others.

I am an Israeli and for us, and for the overwhelming majority of
Israelis, Yom Kippur came very early this year--it came on Rosh Hoashanah
with the news about the massacre of at least 300 Palestinian refugees in
two camps. We responded, and I say "we" advisedly because it was
supporters of the government and opponents of the government alike, and
we said that we know that the people who murdered there call themselves
Christians. Do we have some responsibility for letting them in? Are we
in some way concerned with this? We want to know. We have the moral
responsibility, not to others, but to ourselves. We wish to live in a
society which adopts certain minimum requirements of moral conduct, and
we went into the streets, and some who had influence with the government
went to the government and it took us 10 days and the independent
Committee of Inquiry was set up. But then you look around you in the
world. You look at the reaction of the world. Do they have a right to
this kind of a reaction? Isn't that remindful of what happened 40, 50,
60 years ago? This wave of hatred, when THE NEW YORK TIMES which prints
all the news that is fit to print (and they decide what news is fit to
print) takes two weeks before it comes out with a statement that although
the Israelis are this and that and the other, well, somebody else
actually committed the murder. When the reaction is not only the
throwing of bombs but what is much more dangerous--the writing of articles
in the media, a violent, virulent attack. Was this all about the tragic
event that took place? No, it was triggered by it. It was occasioned
by it. The latent anti-Jewish feelings in societies such as those of
Switzerland, France, Britain, or Italy revealed itself. That reaction
cannot be explained by a massacre conducted by so-called "Christian"
Phalangists in Lebanon. There is a disease there. A deep thorough-

going illness. Who deals with this? I have said repeatedly that
the writers of the books are more dangerous than the throwers of the
bombs. Bombing terrorists can sometimes be treated by a normal or
near-normal police situation. But an intellectual movement is
different. Nazism was an intellectual movement. It started with
articles, with books, mainly with one book, though it was written in
impossible German. Not too many people actually managed to read
through it, but it was a guide. The others followed. It was the
intellectuals amongst the Nazis that made Nazism possible. It was the
German intellectuals who were inducted into the Nazi movement that
made its success possible. I want to emphasize this. It is the
central thing with which we must be concerned. I will never cease
reminding people that there were four Einsatzgruppen, the murder
squads that entered the Soviet Union in June, 1941, and killed 1.4
million Jews, machine gunning them between June 41 and December 42.
Three of these Einsatzgruppen were commanded by PHD's. The people
responsible for the selections in Auschwitz were medical doctors. The
people who were supervising the throwing of gas crystals into the gas
chambers were doctors who had sworn their hippocratic oath. It was
the doctors who supervised medical experiments in the German camps.
They not only supervised, but did them. The first groups to join the
Nazi party were the student organizations of Germany and the teachers'
organizations. Don't forget that. Intellectuals can easily be
swayed. And if you look at the Nazi period, and then you look at our
own period, there are some signs of danger. Do you remember the case
of the frightful cult murder, the suicide in Guyana? Do you
remember who actually prepared the poison for hundreds of people? It
was a physician of that cult who was with them. He received a degree
from an American medical school.

When you look at the media, there is nothing more dangerous.
There is nothing that has better prospects for doing good than the
media. I am told that Americans watch TV 7 hours a day on the average.
I can't imagine how it can be so, but you will remember what Mark
Twain said about this: namely, that there are lies, damn lies, and
statistics, and possibly this particular statistic comes under this
headline. But, it is clear that a lot of Americans watch a lot of TV.
Who controls this? What are the criteria by which these people go?
How do they choose what to represent to the public and what not to
present? Do they have any code of ethics? We can ask about recent
developments, not only regarding the war in Lebanon, but elsewhere, too.
Are there not signs that something is wrong somewhere? The Iraqi-
Iranian war, at least about 130,000 casualties altogether and all we
saw were clips from Iraqi TV. Commentary--none. Why? Does it not
affect the oil supplies of the western world? Should it not stir the
world to action to stop this senseless killing? Or take the war in
Ogaden, between Somalia and Ethopia. Ethiopia is supported by the force

of Soviet arms. Were there any TV crews on the spot to check who
was doing what? What about the mass starvation in the Sahara and around
it? Millions of human beings are dying there. Any report on that? And
I could go on and on and on. Who chooses? And it is not only the
choice, you see. It is how you present commentaries. You have to
balance it. You balance it between Republicans and Democrats, between
one set of diplomats and another set of diplomats, and there is hardly
any discussion. Well, you don't really have too much time for it
because you have to leave time for commercials, otherwise, the TV
station cannot function. That whole situation to me is a sign of a
threat to freedom because, to have your freedom threatened, you don't
have to have a police state. You don't have to have autocratic
government. You can do quite well without them, too. There is every
possibility of the world of completely contorting the picture. That is,
if you have the right media at your disposal, the right sources of
information and the right sources of disinformation. There is a whole
science of disinformation starting with the propaganda of war where
both sides try to introduce lying propaganda in order to confuse the
enemy, and now it is used in peace time. That is one danger of subverting
our society.

Now, there is this business which some people here have already
mentioned: the issue of the denial of the Holocaust. It is something
that concerns me very deeply not only because I happen to be with this
particular subject, but because there is a problem there which goes
deeper than the actual denial of the Holocaust itself. Because, come
to think of it, the Holocaust is unbelievable. I have myself taken
testimony from survivors who, after they had given the testimony, said,
"You know, sometimes I wake up and I don't believe I went through this.
It must have been a nightmare. It was unbelievable." And then, your
son and daughter, whether you are Jewish, or Gentile, American,
Argentinian, French, Italian or Japanese, it makes no difference, comes
and says, Listen, millions of peoples being shoved into the gas chambers
for absolutely no reason at all, just because some pseudo-religious,
anti-Jewish, anti-semitic crazy government--it doesn't stand to reason.
And then somebody comes and says--indeed, this never happened. These
Jews invented it in order to squeeze money out of the West Germans to
re-establish the Jewish world government, just as it says in the
Protocols of the Elders of Zion, from Palestine, or Israel, over the
world at large. That may, to many people, sound more believable. You
know, on the 28th of April, 1945, THE LONDON DAILY MAIL carried a
story. Field Marshall Montgomery's chief of staff, General Templer,
had had a haircut the day before and the barber, a London cockney,
asked him, "Sir, do you really believe in the stories of Bergen Belsen
and Buchenwald?" That was April 28, 17 days after the liberation of
Buchenwald and 13 days after the liberation of Bergen Belsen. "Do
you believe in these stories?", the barber asked. Templer said
"I was aghast. How could you not believe that? Our soldiers went in
and saw it!" and the barber said, "You know, back in Wimbeldon, I
went into the pub on my last leave only two days ago and all my buddies

there said, "It could not have happened." Propaganda. The denial of the Holocaust could turn out to be another version of Goebbels' big lie. The lie that there was no such thing. Which is like saying that Japan does not exist. That the earth if flat. That the sun shines only on Mondays and Thursdays. But, you just try and convince these people. It's a terrible thought because what controls this in the end is certain non-governmental agencies and ways of convincing people.

It is my contention that advocates of totalitarianism on left and right make war on democracy, by attacking the Jews. This is an attack on American democracy for the people in Los Angeles, on French democracy for the people in France, in Sweden they attack the Swedish democracy, in Germany the German Federal Republic, and so on and so forth. It is an attack on the only hope that we have of something better. It is a sign of an intellectual disease. Now, admittedly, democrary is something terrible. To paraphrase Winston Churchill, democracy is indeed the worst system of government, except, of course, for all the other alternatives. And it is that system of government that is being attacked. It is a great compliment for the Jews. They are identified by their opponents with humanism, liberalism. Hitler is quoted as saying that "Conscience is a Jewish invention. It must be done away with." Look at the GESPRACHE MIT HITLER by Herrman Rauschning, published 1939 in London. It is there. When you look at that, you'll see that something new happens, that when you dehumanize a people, you not only dehumanize others but you yourself undergo a process of dehumanization.

However, signs of oppression should not, with all due respect, be the only theme of this conference, because rebellion against oppression and the fight against kinds of oppression is the other side of the coin. I would argue that if this fight was hopeless, if this thing was getting bigger and bigger and there was no future, then what would be the point in making speeches? What would be the point in teaching the Holocaust? What would be the point in all the effort we make? But out of the Holocuast itself comes not only destruction and murder; not only the murder of Jews and murder of millions of others, but also a message of rebellion of a different type. Let me make a few comments on that because I think that this is very important.

You must tell people what the dangers are but if you are convinced that these dangers can be fought, you must give them some tools to fight with. The concentration camps (and I am not talking about the death camps) were established by the Naxis as a system of total dehumanization. One person was set against the other. The actual beatings, the actual torture was done largely by terrorized prisoners on other terrorized prisoners, in this situation of total destruction of humanity. The idea was that everyone should fight everyone and it is no wonder that many succumbed to it. It is no wonder that you had frightful occurrences between the prisoners themselves in the concentration camps. However, this should be seen for what it wanted to achieve: it was a totalitarian system. Because it was a total system, had it failed in only one case, it would have failed because it would not have included the totality of the prisoners who were to be dehumanized. But there was more than one person who stood up against it. There were thousands and tens of thousands. Who knows? Maybe more than that. Maybe hundreds of thousands. They are not with us any more. Those who are, testify that they survived because somebody helped them. They testify that there was tremendous heroism, as well as the opposite phenomenon. If people in that kind of situation were capable of humane action, is not that a rebellion against oppression? Is not that a sign that humanity has some kind of hope? Let me give you well known examples: The great Hebrew and Yiddish poet, Yitzhak Katznelson, in the Warsaw Ghetto, taught classes in an illegal high school in the ghetto. What did he teach them? History, bible, poetry. And he gave them examinations to write with pencil and old cardboard paper and they received grades in accordance with pre-war Polish system of high school matriculation. Crazy? No! This was intended to be one kind of an answer. One kind of an answer to oppression. Janusz Korczak--I don't know what he told the children when he was leaving on the train that brought them to Treblinka. Nobody knows. I don't know whether he told them anything at all, but he and the other teachers went with the children, neatly clad, in good order, with their heads held high. That was all he could do and that is what he did. The affirmation of humanity against a system that tries to dehumanize is the extreme case. In democratic societies today, there are little attempts at dehumanization. They are insignificant events by comparison. We are not facing a Holocaust. We are facing discrimination, prejudice, dangers to a democratic system. The extreme case could teach us something about our relatively wonderfully peaceful life so that we should never have to deal with extreme situations. Even bad people were moved occasionally to do deeds that they had not been prepared to do. I always remember the saying of Confucius that if a robber walks by a small brook and sees a baby fall into the brook and even if he is an arch-criminal, he will jump in to rescue the child. I don't know whether Confucius was right. Who knows? But I do know that the Bulgarian Fascist deputy for the town of Kyustendil was approached by the heads of the Jewish community in that small Bulgarian town in March, 1943, and he was told that the Jews were going to be deported to their death. Do something, they said: and he went to the rostrum of the Bulgarian parliament and he demanded that this should be stopped and others joined him. Fascist deputies, a Fascist king, as well as many opponents of Fascism, and it was prevented. We all know that there are very few Gentiles who helped Jews in Eastern Europe, but there were some. Of course, these are the exceptions but why are the exceptions so important for us? Because it is our task to make these exceptions the rule. Let me end this opening address with a story which I like

to tell because it shows both sides of the picture, in a way.
The founder of Youth Alliyah, that is the program of bringing children
without their parents to Palestine from Germany under the Hitler
regime, was started by the widow of a Berlin Rabbi, Recha Freier,
she is still alive in Jerusalem today. She brought out children, as
many as she could or as the British government in Palestine would
let in, and by the time 1940 came, she knew she had to get out. On
her way, and she had an official entry permit into Palestine, she
passed through Vienna and she took a number of 12 to 14 year old Jewish
girls from Austria with her. She crossed the border into Yugoslavia.
She landed in Zegreb. She tried to get entry for these children into
Palestine and she failed, and she had to go because her visa was
ending and she would lost the opportunity of going, and so she left
the children with a young Jewish youth leader. His name was Josef
Indig, known as Yoshko. Yoshko Indig got these few girls and then
when it spread around that he was dealing with refugees, other children
came and joined the party and then on the 6th of April, 1941, the
Germans marched in. On the 10th of April, they were in Zagreb and
Yoshko with his group fled from Zagreb into the Croatian hills and
there, too, kids from Germany, Austria, refugee kids heard about this
and joined them. He had 149 kids from the ages of 4 to 16 and he was
all of 20 years old. He knew that Croatia was a very bad place to be
in the Spring of 1941, and so he took these kids to Slovenia where
there was Italian occupation and that was more lenient. He got a
Slovenian lady to give her home to these 149 children. Some friendly
Italian soldiers gave him food. Through them, he contacted the
Italian-Jewish community and they supplied him with some money and he
stayed in Lesno Brod in Slovenia from June 1941 to September 1942; he
instituted a rigorous regime of education, sports, Hebrew, singing,
poetry, literature. In September, 1942, the big deportations to
Auschwitz took place and Slovenia became unsafe. Yoshko took his
children in Italian trucks and went to the village of Nonantola in
the Appennines. There, there were two Catholic priests and the local
underground head of the Communist party in the region, and the three
of them kept the 149 children alive in the homes of the villagers of
that place from September 1942 to September 1943, and no Fascist
policeman ever got to know about it. In September, 1943, the Nazis
occupied Italy and Yoshko took trucks which were supplied to him by
the villagers and he loaded his children onto the trucks and he went
up to the Italian borders. It was September, there was already snow,
and they made a long line, the bigger ones carrying the smaller ones
and they crossed through the snow into Switzerland. They reached
Switzerland. In 1945 they reached Palestine. They are all now in
Israel.

Yoshko Indig and his children were the only case of any
children's group that was saved in the Holocaust. The only case. No
other children's group was rescued like this from 1941 to 1945. Yes,
there were children who were saved, brought over the borders to
Switzerland, to Spain. But from 1941 to the end of the Holocaust,
there was one single case of group rescue. There could have been many,

many more. It is a sign of tremendous heroism. A rebellion
against oppression. A different kind of rebellion than that with
which we are normally acquainted. And yet, you see, there was only
one. Had there been more Catholic priests like that, more Communist
party officials like that, more Italian soldiers or soldiers of other
groups of other nations, perhaps had there been more Yoshko Indigs,
there would have been more rescues. Perhaps, also, he was tremendously
lucky. But, you see, there is a hope in the fight against oppression.
There is a hope if people still pull together. If people are not lazy,
if they try to analyze the situation in which they find themselves,
and not leave it to analysis, but then act. Whether it is an education,
whether it is in the media, whether it is in the universities, whether
it is in the professions, to teach humaneness, to try to see this world
which is not going in a very good direction and take the reins in the
hands and try to do something about it. I always thought that the
French philosopher, Descartes, was wrong. You know he said "Cogito,
Ergo Sum" -- I think, therefore I am. No--I fight, therefore, I am.
As long as I fight, I am. The moment I stop fighting, I am not.

THE HOLOCAUST AND GENOCIDE:
SOME PROBLEMS IN INTERPRETATION AND UNDERSTANDING

DR. HUBERT G. LOCKE

In this address, I want to undertake a difficult and what some of
you may find to be an unpopular task, but one that I have come to believe is long overdue. I wish to propose a question that is far greater
in scope or importance than I have the time and perhaps the capacity to
answer. But for reasons I hope to make clear in the course of my remarks, the question can no longer be ignored, nor its answer assumed.
I ask at the outset for your forebearance and your understanding; this
address must be seen as an inquiry-in-progress, not as a finished product.

———————

In Jewish homes, as part of the ancient ritual which commemorates
Pesach or Passover, it is customary for the youngest male to ask the
question: why is this night different from all other nights?

In recent years, I have increasingly felt the need to ask a similar
question with respect to the Holocaust: why is it different--or even
more bluntly stated--is the Holocaust different from all other events
of genocide and other manifestations of human slaughter that mar the
record of modern civilization?

This relatively straightforward query is difficult to pose for two
reasons. First, in non-Jewish circles, the temptation to hyperbole in
the face of any and every phenomenon which we find appalling gives rein
to a looseness in our use of language that often leads to confusion
rather than clarification or illumination of critical events and experiences in our time. Second, in Jewish circles, there is frequently
a commitment to the interpretation of the Holocaust which does not permit, a priori, its discussion or comparison in the context of any other
historical event, no matter how horrendous or devasting its human consequences.

The non-Jewish world may find it emotionally satisfying to apply
the term "holocaust" to all sorts of events--actual or potential--which
terrify the human imagination, while the Jewish community--and especially
the survivors of the virtual destruction of European Jewry--may, more
understandably, wish to insist on an a priori difference between that
event and all other events of human slaughter. However, in the scholarly
community we are obliged to take a more distanced stance and, even at the
risk of being misunderstood in our efforts, nevertheless seek to determine
if the claim of the Holocaust as an event sui generis holds up under
rigorous scrutiny.

The scholarly obligation to press this question, unrestrained by the passions of either position, cannot be overemphasized. I acknowledge at the outset that scholars, too, are not immune from passion, even when it is concealed under the antiseptic cloak of scholarly inquiry. But at its best, scholarly inquiry is a rather precise, time-honoured way of approaching difficult and ofttimes volatile questions and issues with a single-minded determination to uncover and analyze the facts, free of political or ideological commitments or foregone conclusions. Such inquiries mark most of the extant literature on the Holocaust and, to a lesser extent, the literature on genocide; we are long overdue, however, in addressing directly the question of the uniqueness of the Holocaust itself as a central issue.

But there is also a more compelling reason for such an inquiry. The twentieth century has, as one of its defining characteristics, a tragic series of episodes of human slaughter, so much so in fact that our century has been termed the century of genocide.

Ours is an era in which the capacity of nations and societies to engage in the most barbaric of social pathologies seems to know no limits. If we are ever to understand this darker side of human experience, to curb its expression or to guard against its reoccurrence, then we need desperately to weigh the Holocaust against all other genocides and to attempt to discover whether it constituted an aberration in the history of Western society, or another in a long chain of similar events, or whether it was an occurrence sufficiently unique to warrant a specialized attention and a particular dread.

If the Holocaust is ultimately seen as a unique event--not an historical aberration or one in a long history of similar events--then our efforts to understand, first Germany in that critical period of the waning years of the Weimar Republic and the subsequent twelve year period of the Third Reich, then how such an unspeakable atrocity as the Final Solution came to be conceived and implemented and why some of the countries which fell under Nazi domination eagerly joined in the execution of that Final Solution while others resisted; if we are to comprehend the mixed record of the neutral nations in the face of the reality which was unfolding regarding the plight of Europe's Jewish populace and especially if we are to understand why the rest of the "civilized" Western world sat in virtual silence in the face of mounting, documented reports of the Jewish slaughter, acting only after it was almost too late to stem the tide of destruction--all these factors and circumstances take on an even heightened importance. But the task properly begins with a dispassionate attempt to answer the question: was the Holocaust another in a long and tragic series of episodes of human madness, or is there something in that event which sets it apart from all other occurrences of genocide and human destruction?

II

In this address, I do not propose to answer this critical question;

it obviously constitutes an inquiry of many years duration. I believe the question suggests, however, the next stage in Holocaust research which ought to be undertaken--a careful and comparative sifting of the historical records of this century's genocides and the development of a taxonomy or a framework for analysis that would permit us to discern and describe the distinctive features of these occurrences.

Regrettably, the twentieth century gives us much material with which to work. There is the slaughter of some 600,000 to 800,000 Armenians by the Ottoman regime in Turkey during the first World War, an act which many scholars consider the first genocide of this century. There is the fate of some estimated twenty million ethnic Russians during the Stalin era who were systematically rounded up, transported, and starved to death in Soviet gulags. More recently, there is the human tragedy that befell the Biafrans in Nigeria who died in the hundreds of thousands at the hands of a hostile government in power, or the widespread extermination of Tibetans who have suffered a similar fate following the invasion of that tiny nation by the People's Republic of China. And if we step back a century in time, we have only to inquire into the reduction of the Native American population in our country, from an estimated three million to less than a half million people, in order to contemplate our own sorry history in this regard.

The very enumeration, however, reflects in part the nature of the problem we face in any attempt to sort and classify those events, particularly if we turn to the literature for guidance. Two brief quotations may help to make this point clear:

First, a volume entitled War Crimes and Genocide, published in 1972, opens with the following paragraph:

"This age of violence has been witness to some of the most gruesome crimes against humanity--bombing of cities of Hiroshima and Nagasaki; death in the gas chamber by the millions; the horrors of the concentration camps and the war in Viet Nam. But the devastation and misery wrought on the people of Bangla Desh by the Pakistani Army is the most horrifying.... The military Junta of Pakistan committed atrocities in Bangla Desh that have no parallel in world history."

The second quotation is from the incisive but problematic essay on Genocide by Irving Louis Horowitz, published in 1976. He quotes, as an illustration of the genocidal norm in the twentieth century, from an article by Leon Gordenker:

"Who made the destruction of the 300,000 or so Indonesian communists after the attempted coup d'etat in 1965 a matter for the United Nations? Who saw the deprivation of the rights of Asians in Uganda as an outrage? Who labeled as genocidal the slaughter of ba Hutu tribesmen--80,000 or so of them--by the wa Tusi elite of Burundi? How much attention was given to the horrors of the civil war in Nigeria?"

"If candor is to prevail," Horowitz concludes, "statesmen and scholars alike would have to admit that the unbilical cord between genocidal practice and state power has never been stronger" (pp. 20-21).

At the risk of offending those who have every right to feel passionately about these other horrendous occurrences of human slaughter, I nevertheless believe that they reflect an undiscerning amalgamation of the terrible and the barbaric which does not permit us to identify and locate the sources of human barbarism in the careful and precise manner in which, for example, we have learned to diagnose physical diseases in the medical sciences. All disease is horrible, to be sure, but some diseases are more horrible than others. Equally important, we do not cure disease in general; our century has made enormous strides in modern health because we have learned to identify and isolate particular diseases and their causes and to search for the remedies and antidotes appropriate to a given malady. We face in this century's human slaughters a monumental societal disease; I believe we face in the Holocaust a particular and peculiar manifestation of that disease which requires a specialized attention to its isolation and diagnosis.

III

In trying, therefore, to make some sense from a modern history that is replete with accounts of the unnatural deaths of massive numbers of people, I wish only to suggest, in the remainder of this address, the broad outlines that such an inquiry might take. I begin with the definitional distinction on which my colleague, Professor Lyman Legters, insists and one that I believe is critical. Legters holds that we should observe the basic distinction between genocidal--or those acts which tend toward or which may result in genocide--and genocide itself, or the deliberate and systematic destruction of a racial, political or cultural group. This distinction, while it may seem obvious, would--if observed--clean up a great deal of the rhetorical looseness in our contemporary discussions.

It is the failure to observe this distinction, for example, that makes Professor Horowitz' otherwise brilliant essay so problematic. Horowitz has done much to aid our understanding of the many cultural and political forms which genocide has taken in the 20th century; he cites, however, South Africa as a nation in which "the minority... practices a form of genocide on the majority" (p.18), the Dutch-run slave trade (p.19) and the generalized violence in the nation of Columbia throughout most of this century (pp.48-49)--all as varying forms of genocide. Horowitz is precise in his definition of genocide as "a structural and systematic destruction of innocent people by a state bureaucratic apparatus" (p.18) but his illustrations range over such a wide and varied tapestry of human barbarism that we are left

without any clear distinctions that would enable us to say whether all
of these experiences must be seen simply as gross examples of human
barbarity or whether there are salient elements which distinguish one
barbarity from another.

To return for a moment to the Legters' distinction, whether particular occurrences of human slaughter can be termed as genocidal or as
actual acts of genocide, become important differentiations. Massive
numbers of Japanese citizens died in the bombings of Hiroshima and Nagasaki, some 15,000 Polish troops were estimated to have been destroyed
by the Red Army in the infamous Katyn Forest Massacre, and the fire
bombing of Dresden resulted in massive slaughter of German civilians.
As tragic as each of these occurrences were, and as frequent as they
appear in the literature as acts of genocide, it is difficult to con-
ceive of them either as acts of genocide or even as genocidal; no one
suggests that they were deliberately or systematically conceived and
carried out in order to destroy an entire racial, political, or cultural
group. Likewise, what our nation did in Viet Nam, with what Horowitz
terms "its mortifying tenets of death through air attacks, including
napalm and jelly bombings and the wide use of chemical defoliants"
(p.55) which led such eminent critics of the war as Jean Paul Sartre
and Hugo Bedau to describe that war as a case of genocide, may in fact
be considered as genocidal but not of the authentic dimensions of genocide.

In these events of human slaughter just recited, we begin to get
several important clues for our inquiry. Although we must acknowledge
the degree to which such a distinction is subject to abuse, there would
seem to be some warrant for distinguishing large-scale occurrences of
human slaughter which take place in the course of a military conflict
from other events of mass human destruction. We sense also the significance of scope in our analysis; no one would be so foolish as to propose
a body count in order to establish the significance of the event--never-
theless, genocide is defined as having as its aim the destruction of most or
all of a racial, political or cultural group (the Holocaust was clearly
aimed at the entire elimination of the Jewish people). Further, Horowitz does offer us a useful defining characteristic of genocide by
pointing to the necessity of such events occurring under auspices and
with the approval of the formal machinery of a government, as distinct
from the random or sporadic activity of persons or groups who have
neither legitimate power nor standing in a political system. Finally,
we sense the importance of intent--a deliberately conceived, designed,
and implemented effort to destroy a racial, political or cultural group.

If we can distinguish, therefore, between the countless acts of
human slaughter that have occurred in this century, laying aside for
the moment our great fear about that potential act of destruction
which nuclear warfare presents and which some insist is the only
"holocaust" worthy of our current consideration, and if we can separate
out those past events that were genocidal in character in order to

concentrate our attention on those occurrences which may be considered as actual acts of genocide, we narrow the scope of our inquiry considerably.

I believe we will move even closer to the answer to the query that I have raised if we take into the framework of our analysis the following additional questions. First, what is the socio-economic climate in which acts of genocide have been conceived and planned? Second, what political mobilization has been mounted in order to carry out an act of genocide? Third, what is the distinctive nature of the ideology-- the set of beliefs and values--which fuels and drives an act of genocide? Fourth, to what extent is the act of genocide an integral part of a plan of military expansion and conquest or an act which is carried out in defiance of military objectives? Finally, what institutions in a society either restrain or enhance the implementation of the genocidal act?

No less an interpreter of the Holocaust than Elie Wiesel has insisted that "the universality of the Holocaust must be realized in its uniqueness. This problem," he states as he reported on the trip of the President's Commission on the Holocaust to Auschwitz and other death camps,"...this problem--how to reconcile the specifically Jewish victims with the universality of all victims--haunted us throughout the pilgrimage."

It is this very problem which I am suggesting that we turn our attention to in a rigorous, systematic way. I number myself among those who believe that we face in the Holocaust a unique and unparalleled event in history; we must, however, make that uniqueness explicit by its comparison with other events of mass slaughter--prepared to abandon our belief if it proves unsupportable but if it is supportable, then we must redouble our efforts to address those particular pathologies which brought it about, in order to insure that it and anything remotely resembling it, never occurs again.

THE OBLIGATION OF A LAW SCHOOL TO INSTRUCT STUDENTS IN MORALITY

DEAN J. WILLARD O'BRIEN

I wish first to acknowledge my debt to Dorothy Freedman who invited me to attend and to participate in this year's annual Conference on the Holocaust. I was privileged to take part in last year's Conference as well. These two experiences have forced me to think through some familiar problems in the context of a precise event--the Holocaust, an event that I admit with considerable regret I had not truly focused on in a careful and deliberate manner. As a result, I have learned much. For that I am most grateful.

I have titled my remarks "The Obligation of a Law School to Instruct Students in Morality." I shall not speak here about courses in Professional Responsibility which deal with traditional ethical problems of lawyers within the profession. I might add that the Villanova Law School has from its inception required students to take instruction in Legal Ethics. I shall not in these remarks speak further about the Villanova Law School except to say that it is, of course, an extraordinarily fine school.

My topic addresses a concern which is more fundamental than the traditional Professional Responsibility course. I will start with a few observations made by a man trained in the law at a superb law school, a man who later in life served as a friend and confidant of a President of the United States, a man who himself sought unsuccessfully that same high office. The man, the Honorable Sargent Shriver, the President, John Fitzgerald Kennedy.

Mr. Shriver spoke in the Rockefeller Chapel at the University of Chicago on Sunday, October 22, 1978. His words showed surprise, sadness and perhaps resignation:

I went to Yale Law School in 1938 naively expecting to study about justice...what was right and wrong; what ought to be done to improve society; how to extend the writ of law to overcome the inequities of life. Did I get a shock! The Professors told me the law had little or nothing to do with justice. What the judge ate for breakfast had more to do with his rulings than legal precedents... Oliver Wendell Holmes' famous dicta were almost holy writ. Holmes had written concerning the law that there was 'no brooding omnipresence in the sky'-- no law that transcended the particularities of cases which were to be decided on pragmatic, social mores grounds.

* * * *

"When persons in our society reach a certain level in business, law, medicine, politics, education and other professions, many of the problems they face are moral problems. For the person who becomes President of the United States nearly all the problems are moral problems. Rarely, if ever, does the President lack for military advice, scientific advice, financial advice, medical advice, female advice, Chicano advice, Black advice, or diplomatic advice. He just can't get the advice he needs the most."

Have things changed? Mr. Shriver went to the Yale Law School in 1938. In 1978, 40 years later, Roger C. Crampton, then Dean of the Cornell Law School, wrote an article entitled "The Ordinary Religion of the Law School Classroom." (29 Journal of Legal Education 247) As the title suggests, Dean Crampton was concerned about the "fundamental value assumptions" of law professors and law students. He wrote:

"The essential ingredients of the ordinary religion of the American law school classroom are: a skeptical attitude toward generalizations; an instrumental approach to law, and lawyering; a 'tough-minded' and analytical attitude toward legal tasks and professional roles; and a faith that man, by the application of his reason and the use of democratic processes, can make the world a better place." (p.248)

The first of those ingredients, "a skeptical attitude toward generalizations," involves the denial of the existence of a God or at least the relevance of God to the legal system. Under that ingredient

"There is no 'brooding omnipresence' from which principles or rules can be derived. Law is not a logical system in which a rule to be applied to a new situation is deduced by logic from some fundamental, pre-existing principle." (pp. 248-249)

* * * *

"From a realistic standpoint, law is merely what officials of the law do." (p. 249)

As for the second ingredient, namely, the instrumental approach to law taken in law schools, the result is that "since the lawyer is engaged in the implementation of the values of others—a client or a government agency or the general society—he need not be concerned directly with value questions." (p.250) Because of the tough-minded, analytical attitude adopted by law professors, i.e., the third ingredient, "two models of professional behavior are presented to law students: the 'hired gun' and the 'social engineer'.... The hired gun gets his goals from the client he serves; the social engineer either prefabricates his own goals or gets them from the interests he serves." (p.251)

According to Dean Crampton, not much has changed in the 40 plus years that have elapsed since Sargent Shriver first arrived at the Yale Law School, a fact that concerned Dean Crampton:

> "The aim of all education, even in a law school, is to encourage a process of continuous self-learning that involves the mind, spirit and body of the whole person. This cannot be done unless larger questions of truth and meaning are directly faced." (p. 263)

The problems are not being faced directly or otherwise except by a relatively few professors dedicated to the task of righting the situation. The task is formidable. The courses necessary to even begin dealing with the larger questions of truth are not in the law school curriculum and the students surmise from that omission, and correctly so, that law professors who created the curriculum believe that those issues are unimportant to the practice of law.

I would like to place the issue in larger perspective.

I am certain that if one were to ask the people of this country whether the source of those "inalienable rights" of life, liberty and the pursuit of happiness was some form of natural law or a Divine Being or whether they were given and could properly be taken away by whatever group of men happened to control our civil law, the overwhelming majority would respond that those inalienable rights had as their source God, not men. Yet, if you were to ask those same people whether commonly held religious beliefs could properly be considered when making law, I suspect that many, and perhaps most, would say that our common beliefs could not be considered.

If we were to accept the notion that our legal system is, has always been and must always be a purely secular system that requires the elimination of all thoughts about a Divine Being in its administration, then today, we could not write the Declaration of Independence, draft the United States Constitution, or officially state the preamble to the Constitution of the Commonwealth of Pennsylvania. A purely secular system would not permit the declaration that "...all men...are endowed by their Creator with certain inalienable Rights...." The "Blessings of Liberty" referred to in the preamble to the Constitution of the United States have as their source one of those inalienable, God-given rights, namely Liberty. It is clear that the Preamble to the Constitution of the Commonwealth of Pennsylvania could not be written in a purely secular legal system. It states, "We, the people of the Commonwealth of Pennsylvania, grateful to Almighty God for the blessings of civil and religious liberty, and humbly invoking His guidance, do ordain and establish this Constitution."

Professor Harold Berman of the Harvard Law School has summarized the history of the secularization of legal education this way:

"In the past two generations the public philosophy of
America has shifted radically from a religious to a secular
theory of law, from a moral to a political or instrumental
theory, and from a communitarian to an individualistic
theory. Law is now generally considered--at least in public
discourse--to be simply a pragmatic device for accomplishing
specific political, economic, and social objectives. Its
tasks are thought to be finite, material, impersonal--to get
things done, to make people act in certain ways. Rarely, if
ever, does one hear it said that law is a reflection of an
objective justice or of the ultimate meaning or purpose of
life. Usually it is thought to reflect, at best, the community's sense of what is expedient, and more commonly, the
more or less arbitrary will of the lawmaker."

As Professor Berman states, our entire society has become
secularized at least on the issue of the relationship between God's
law and man's law.

I will share with you an experience I had this past summer. A
committee of the American Bar Association held hearings in Philadelphia on the issue whether the American Bar Association should accredit
the new law school at Oral Roberts University. The problem arose because the law school requires all prospective students and faculty
members to sign an oath to follow a particular religious belief--a
fundamentalist Christian belief. Catholics, Jews and many others
would not be admitted as students or hired as law professors.

Among those who appeared in opposition to the accreditation of
the law school was a representative of the Anti-Defamation League of
B'nai B'rith. He began his statement by pointing out that "The Anti-
Defamation League was organized in 1913 to advance goodwill and mutual
understanding among Americans of all creeds and races and to combat
racial and religious prejudice in the United States" and that the
Anti-Defamation League opposed "in the most vigorous terms the accreditation of the (law school) at Oral Roberts University, a law school
which requires a religious test--indeed it includes a religious oath--
for admission of students and employment of faculty."

The opposition of the Anti-Defamation League was quite understandable and the arguments made were quite moving. What I wish to convey
to you today is the way the representative viewed professional education.
He said, and I quote:

"Schools devoted to religious studies could still limit
faculty positions and student admissions in particularly
sectarian types of courses of study, e.g., seminaries. They
may practice their religion as they see fit; they may not however, engage in religious discrimination in administering
secular academic programs such as law, medicine or engineering.

"The ABA's standard would be providing a preference to religious groups which is not available to other groups. In seminary settings, this establishment clause violation would be outweighed by free exercise interests; but that is not true in the secular setting of a law school....Preferences cannot be granted to religious groups when they themselves choose to become involved in the primarily secular activity of operating law schools, which are not essentially religious in nature."

The observation I wish to make is that the representative of the Anti-Defamation League hammered away at the point that professional training is a secular enterprise. If, as I believe, the representative is a lawyer, that would not be surprising because that is what he was taught at whatever law school he studied.

Permit me to share with you one more observation, this one from the pen of a pyschologist-philosopher (Frederick A. Elliston). Bar Examiners are people whose function it is, among other things, to determine whether a prospective lawyer is "of good moral character," a difficult task at best. A series of papers appeared recently in a magazine written for Bar Examiners. (The Bar Examiner, Vol. 51, No. 3 August 1982) In one of those papers the psychologist-philosopher questioned whether we should even try to determine whether would-be lawyers are "of good moral character." Why? Listen to what he wrote. Perhaps I should add that he wrote in broad strokes deliberately to provoke, but he wrote what he believes. I quote:

"Now one can debate at length what makes someone a morally good person. Most of the discussions have focused on this issue.

* * * *

"All these debates are beside the point, however, if the principle of identity is false. If it is not necessary to be a morally good person in order to be a good lawyer, if indeed it is sometimes a hindrance, then moral fitness tests are pointless. I believe that the identity principle is false. In its place I shall offer two others:

P^2 That a good lawyer is sometimes immoral.

P^3 That a good lawyer is amoral.

The recent literature on the professional responsibilities of lawyers attempts to work out a professional ethics for lawyers. In so doing many legal scholars have further challenged the assumption that a good lawyer is a good person. Perhaps the most famous (or infamous) example of this is Monroe Freedman. In a groundbreaking article he argued that a lawyer

must put his client on the stand knowing that he intends
to commit perjury. By ordinary moral standards it is wrong
to lie and to help others to lie. Yet Freedman's lawyer
would permit it and perhaps by his silence facilitate his
client's lying.

"Similarly, it is ordinarily wrong to prevent others
from discovering the truth. Yet in the celebrated Garrow
case, the lawyer, who knew where the two bodies were buried
and deliberately did not tell, has been defended by writers
and exonerated by the New York State Bar.

"Ordinarily it is wrong to harm innocent people. But
if a defense attorney can discredit a truthful rape victim's
testimony, because she is emotionally distraught, the Code
of Professional Responsibility would enjoin to do so.

"These examples can be multiplied, qualified and questioned. But the fact that actions ordinarily judged wrong
are defended by legal scholars challenges the testing of a
candidate for their adherence to ordinary moral principles.

"No doubt many would like to dismiss these examples as
aberrations, exceptions to the rule that good lawyers are
good people. But I do not think they are exceptions. For
the roots of the lawyer's moral obligation is in his duty
to represent his client's interests zealously within the
limits of the law. However one quibbles over the qualifica-
tion 'zealously,' the point remains that the primary con-
straint on the lawyer's action is the law and not morality--
certainly not his own morality, nor the community's morality,
nor any general or ordinary morality, except insofar as
these have been enacted into law."

What we end up with is frightening. A secular society, law training
primarily as a secular enterprise, and lawyers as people whose work requires them sometimes to be immoral and at best amoral. This is what
the law--man's law--commands. In all this I see the possibility of
another Holocaust. It might not be the Jews next time, but it could be.

My dictionary defines secular as "of or relating to the worldly
or temporal." Temporal is defined as "of or relating to earthly life."
If all these people are right, we are training lawyers to follow the
law, the will of the civil authority, and withholding from them instruction in morality, as that word is used in the Judeo-Christian tradition.

What is the consequence of a person saying that the teaching of law
is primarily a secular endeavor. If we agree that it is a secular effort,
then all value judgments are to be based on the social consensus. A
majority, however designated, imposes its will. That will is not determined

by divine law or immutable laws and is, therefore, changeable. If a particular group becomes unpopular in a purely secular society, the majority can define them out of "humankind" and kill them. It would do no good to claim, in a purely secular state, that a person's right to life comes from God.

Our response to all this might be, change the curriculum in our law schools, instruct our lawyers in morality, make certain that they never could--as the German lawyers did--simply follow the will of the civil lawmakers and permit millions of innocents to be murdered.

Can the course of study be changed? In American law schools academic policies, including the curriculum, are established by the faculties of those schools. Those people are already there. We know how they feel about instructing students in morality in a religious sense. They are opposed to it.

Perhaps in the long run schools can hire people who are interested in the Judeo-Christian concepts of morality. New faculty are hired only with the approval of existing faculty and we know how they feel about the issue. And, of course, even if a school hired someone who claimed to follow the Judeo-Christian tradition, once hired the policy of academic freedom would permit the new faculty member to adopt a contrary position.

Even beyond all this, if a school did hire a faculty committed to instruct in the moral principles found in the Judeo-Christian tradition, which principles would all of us agree on, if any? Those of us who share the Judeo-Christian tradition have a most destructive trait. We race instantly to those issues which divide us instead of concentrating on those things which bind us together. Rabbi Morris N. Keitzer has written: "Christians and Jews share the same rich heritage of the Old Testament with its timeless truths and its unchanging values. They share their belief in the fatherhood of one God--all-knowing, all powerful, ever-merciful, the God of Abraham, Isaac and Jacob. They share their faith in the sanctity of the Ten Commandments, the wisdom of the prophets, and the brotherhood of man."

"Central to both faiths is the firm belief...in the imperishable nature of man's soul." (Roston, Religions of America, p. 144 (1975))

With that in mind I wish, in conclusion, to make a modest proposal. Let us agree now on just five principles: (1) the right to life, yours and mine, comes from God; (2) the right to be free, yours and mine, comes from God; (3) the right to speak our minds comes from God; (4) the right to gather with our friends to protest government action comes from God; (5) the right to acquire such property, at least, that is required to provide necessities for ourselves and our families, comes from God. Then let us join together and, whenever, and however possible, remind the professionals that beyond their training is a higher order which must always be obeyed.

And now I end with the beginning, that is, with Mr. Raskin's opening address. Journalists can, in the effort to make this society more
just, serve us particularly well. The print and electronic media can,
if they will, lead the way. They have the power to create a climate
within which the Holocaust could not easily be repeated. They also
have the power to do the opposite.

GENOCIDE AND THE LAW: GERMAN ARYANISM, AMERICAN
SLAVERY, AND SOUTH AFRICAN APARTHEID:
SIMILARITIES AND DIFFERENCES

JUDGE A. LEON HIGGINBOTHAM, JR.

I am keenly aware that many participants in this Holocaust Conference
have devoted substantial portions of their careers and lives in exploring
the traumatic facts, the horrors, the significance, and the implications
of the Holocaust. I will leave it to those scholars to present the more
learned discourses on this subject. I have come this morning looking at
these events through a different lens, as one whose primary focus through
research and writing has been on slavery and the American legal process.
As I have pursued that intriguing corridor in American history, I have
often wondered about the similarities and differences between those events
in our nation two centuries ago, whereby under the rule of law slavery was
sanctioned, and the subsequent tragic events of the 1930's and '40's in
Germany where such pervasive cruelty was practiced and where the total extermination of the Jews and others was sought. Finally, as I have witnessed the partial curtailment of American racism and the defeat of
Hitler and the Third Reich, I have seen rise on the continent of Africa
a powerful nation which has exemplified qualities inherent in the oppression of Jews decades ago in Germany and of Blacks centuries ago in America.
Thus, I have often wondered about the similarities and differences between
the current events in South Africa, as Blacks there confront that nation's
pernicious oppression with those acts of cruelty which Germany imposed on
Jews and the United States earlier imposed on Blacks, while the leaders of
each of these nations proclaimed they were enforcing the legitimate rules
of law in their countries.

When I received this coveted invitation, I pondered over several
questions: On what rationale does one isolate the Holocaust or even the
concept of genocide, as separate issues for sustained and specific inquiries?
Surely one could respond that there are many extensive injustices throughout
the world and that, as human beings, all of us should be concerned about substantial injustices wherever they appear or whatever causes them.

We know that tonight millions of people will go to sleep hungry and
in despair, and some will die before the morning sunrise because of starvation, inadequate health care and malnutrition. Millions have either no
shelter or inhumanely inadequate housing. Throughout the globe, millions
have no realistic basis to believe that during their entire lifetime they
will be able to escape the ravages of massive poverty: they will see
their children ill from acute malnutrition, many of their neighbors and
friends die of starvation, others will linger with debilitating illnesses
which medical science developed cures for decades ago. Thus, millions of
people throughout the globe live in a world which says daily that though
you are not at fault, and though in theory as a human being you have dignity
and are entitled to certain fundamental decency, nevertheless you shall never

be able to escape your miserable plight and despair, even though with the enormous resources of this world, no human being need live in such misery.

Yet, despite our concern about the poverty and human degradation throughout the world, we must recognize that genocide and the Holocaust exemplify an even far more horrendous level of oppression and the absolute worst qualities of mankind. Genocide is not some mere inadequate callousness whereby individuals or nations fail to more equitably distribute resources. Genocide is a deliberate and higher level of malevolence; by definition it is intentional, premeditated, malicious—a willful, deliberate design for the destruction and the dissolution, in part or completely, of a culture and people. It destroys hope and in some instances leads to massive killing of those who are members of the "unwanted" group.

Thus, we meet here today for the Eighth Conference, hoping that other people throughout the world are also meeting so that collectively we shall never forget the Holocaust and that all of us shall seek to understand the implications of genocide and the Holocaust. In the epigraph of his moving classic, "The Rise and Fall of the Third Reich," William L. Shirer quotes George Santayana that "those who do not remember the past are condemned to relive it." This dramatic warning also appears on a plaque on the walls of Auschwitz. In his epigraph, Shirer also quotes Hans Frank, Governor-General of Poland, who said before he was hanged at Nuremberg: "A thousand years will pass and the guilt of Germany will not be erased."

Presumably we meet here today recognizing that mankind should never erase from its memory the guilt of those treacherous years. It is a warning to all of us as to what can be the most vile nature of man. For Germany, a civilization which had produced great artists, musicians, scientists, industrialists, and philosophers, also produced ruthless mass murderers. We meet here to make certain that those who have the prejudices which led to Auschwitz shall be deterred. We must ask probing questions about the nature of man so that we will not unwittingly create or tolerate another monster like Hitler who may fool many because he (or she) speaks first of law and order, but as support grows, uses patent fascist methods to bring about the denigration and even destruction of those who are perceived to be different.

Within this context this morning, I would like to discuss genocide and the law: German aryanism, American slavery and South African apartheid similarities and differences.

With all the other injustices in the world, I know that some will ask, why do you focus only on Germany, the United States and South Africa? I would be the first to admit that there are other spots on the globe where the conduct of nations or groups of people may be so pernicious that it also breaches the precepts outlined by the Anti-Genocide Treaty. But since we have less than an hour, it is not inappropriate to look at only three nations on three separate continents, and to ask historically what have been the similarities and the differences, what lessons should we learn so that in the words of George Santayana, we shall never relive the past.

1. Definition of Genocide--A Broad View

The term "genocide," invented in 1943 as a concept to describe the emerging horror of the Nazi Holocaust, is commonly thought, due to the climate of its creation, to refer to the practice of mass killing alone. It seems, however, that the creator of the term, Raphael Lemkin, perceived a broader meaning for his new word which encompassed the entire process of the destruction of a particular group, whether on racial, religious, ethnic or national grounds. This process could take the form of the eradication of the essence of the group's identity by destroying their cultural, institutional and social framework, by reducing the group to humiliation, poverty, even slavery, by attacking ultimately the most basic aspect of their existence: their lives. Lemkin first used the term in his book, Axis Rule in Occupied Europe (1943) to describe Hitler's invasion and elimination of national and ethnic groups, His broader vision of the term "genocide" is demonstrated by his use of the experience of the Poles to provide an example of the practice, in which he includes: "the destruction of the institutions of self-government,...disrupting the social cohesion of the nation involved and killing or removing elements such as the intelligentsia,...destroying cultural institutions,...interfering with the churches, and so forth." (Yehuda Bauer, "Genocide: Was it the Nazis' Original Plan?," Annals of the American Academy of Political and Social Science..., 450 (July, 1980), p.44.)

By 1947, genocide had become a crime against humanity recognized in law. It "constituted one of the major charges before the International Military Tribunal (IMT) at Nuremberg and of the subsequent 12 trials conducted before United States Military Tribunals in that city." (Robert Wolfe, "Putative Threats to National Security as a Nuremberg Defense for Genocide," Annals of the American Academy of Political and Social Science, 450 (July, 1980), p.47.)

The international rules establishing the I.M.T., and under which the Nuremberg Trials were conducted, defined "crimes against humanity" as atrocities or offenses including, but not limited to, murder, extermination, enslavement, deportation. . .or other inhuman acts committed against any civilian population, or persecutions on political, racial or religious grounds whether or not in violation of domestic laws of the country where perpetrated. (Id. at pp.53-4.) This definition, again, is not exhaustive and is, by no means, restricted to the actual taking of life; it encompasses various acts which aim at the degradation and dehumanization of a group without requiring that their physical existence by destroyed.

In the aftermath of the Nuremberg Trials, the United Nations General Assembly adopted the Convention on the Prevention and Punishment of the Crime of Genocide in 1948 which outlawed under international law the intentional destruction of racial, ethnic, national and religious groups. Article 2 of the Genocide Convention defines "genocide" as:

724. Art. 2 of the Genocide Convention defines
     "genocide" as any of the following acts
     committed with intent to destroy, in whole

or in part, a national, ethnical, racial or
religious group, as such:

(a) Killing members of the group;

(b) Causing serious bodily or mental harm
to members of the group;

(c) Deliberately inflicting on the group
conditions of life calculated to bring
about its physical destruction in whole
or in part;

(d) Imposing measures intended to prevent
births within the group;

(e) Forcibly transferring children of the
group to another group.

(Myres S. McDougal, Harold D. Lasswell, and Ling-chu Chen, Human Rights
and World Public Order (1980), p. 335.) Also in "Human Rights," Dept. of
State, Selected Documents, No. 5 (Mar. 17, 1977), p.7.

Here again, killing is but one of the acts envisaged in the definition; sections b)-d) cover the cultural destruction of the group in terms
of its psychological and physical well-being and includes a fundamental
attack on its being by interfering with its right to self-perpetuation.

A further insight into the broad view of "genocide" is offered by
Lev. E. Dobriansky in his article, "Genocide, the Convention and Politics"
(Ukrainian Quarterly, 1978, 34 (1): pp.31-39.) The writer was a colleague
of Raphael Lemkin in his efforts to achieve ratification of the Convention,
and has continued to work toward this aim over the past 30 years. In analyz-
ing what he perceives as religious genocide in the Ukraine in the form of
Stalin's liquidation of the Ukrainian Orthodox and Churches, he includes
mass deportations, and incarcerations as part of the concept of genocide
in that, although not directly resulting in death, they constitute the
"genocide of the soul of a nation."

2. Aryanism, Slavery, Apartheid--Law as an Instrument of Oppression

The Nazi Holocaust in Hitler's Germany provides an example of the
full definition of genocide, involving a program to annihilate a people,
body and soul. The process included several stages; firstly, that of
humiliation and degradation intended to break the spirit of the group and
dehumanize them. This was achieved by excluding them from the mainstream
of society and relegating them to an ostracized and inferior position
through a denial of civil and political rights, and direct attacks on
their cultural identity. The law was used as a vital tool in this process.

Psychological and physical destruction was then continued by the use of enslavement, torture and beatings. The final stage was bodily annihilation of a great number of the group in concentration camp executions.

The role of law in this process creates a response of horror since that which we hope will protect justice, right and human dignity was used to perpetrate that vilest of crimes against humanity: genocide. One lesson of the Holocaust is surely that whenever we see the law operating as a tool of oppression to deny the cultural identity and human rights of a group, we should be aware of the broader definition of genocide, and remember the end to which such misuse of law led in Germany.

In examining the role of law in perpetuating the institution of slavery in America, striking parallels appear in many areas of legislation designed to repress and degrade the negro population.

The events of the Holocaust, and of American slavery, demonstrate the use of law as an instrument of oppression, to degrade and destroy the body and soul of a culture perpetrated by a ruling group which considers itself racially superior against a different racial group. The analyses of these two historical periods should serve to make us ever aware of the patterns of calculated oppression through law, and the relationship between those patterns and the concept of genocide. An analysis of the South African system will show that the evils of oppressive regimes bent on destruction of cultural identity of an internal group cannot simply be regretted as blemishes on mankind's history, but that "crimes against humanity" continue to be committed in our contemporary world, and furthermore, they occur, not through mere inadvertence, but by the deliberate design of those who have control over law and legal institutions.

The main body of Judge Higginbotham's speech consisted of an examination of this "deliberate design," that is, the calculated use of law by a ruling elite to create an oppressive regime aimed at the degradation, ostracism and destruction of a particular group. In order to emphasize the recurrence of this process throughout history and in today's world, a comparison was made between the legislation of American Slavery, South African apartheid, and that of Hitler's anti-Jewish campaign during the 1930's. The Judge then gave a comparative analysis of the denial of civil and political rights as a method of excluding a group from the mainstream of society and reducing them to a position of subjugation, with a focus upon such areas as rights citizenship and voting, education, marriage, labor and freedom of assembly and association. By way of specific example, he compared the use of "pass laws" requiring identification documents in all three regimes which provides a means to restrict free movement and also to single out and humiliate slaves in America,[1] Jews in Nazi Germany,[2] and non-whites in South Africa.[3]

---

1. 1712 South Carolina statute, Statutes at Large of South Carolina, Vol. 7, p. 352.

2. "Third Notice Regarding Identification Cards," (July 23, 1983, RGBL, I, p. 922.)

3. Bantu (Abolition of Passes and Co-ordination) Act, 1952.

A further example of this process is provided by legislation in all three regimes restricting inter-marriage. In this area, the bigotry of the elite is revealed in full force. In Nazi Germany, the preamble of a 1935 statute prohibiting both marriage and extra-marital relations between Jews and "persons of German or cognate blood," states in the preamble that its purpose is "to conserve the purity of German Blood."[4] In a Virginia statute of 1691, forbidding inter-marriage between any white and any negro, mulatto or Indian, the preamble reflects a stunning similarity in theme to the German act, it states as its purpose the prevention "of that abominable and spurious issue...by negroes, mulattoes and indians intermarrying with english or other white women."[5] In South Africa, the "Prohibition of Mixed Marriages Act" forbidding marriages between a European and a non-European, the latter referring basically to Black Africans and Asian Indians, echoes the same refrain.[6]

3. America's Shame--The Unratified Genocide Convention*

The lessons of history stand clearly before us. The tragedies of American slavery and the Nazi Holocaust provide us with blueprints for observation of the law as an instrument of cultural oppression; with such examples as the brutality of man as ever-present reminders of the possibility of genocidal destruction, we are surely armed with sufficient signals that such horrors should not be allowed to happen again. South Africa, however, provides just one example of the world's failure to prevent the repetition of the patterns of history. From this standpoint, America's failure to ratify the 1948 Convention on the Prevention and Punishment of the Crime of Genocide casts serious doubt on her commitment to the defense of human rights, in that surely the most basic human right is the right to life, and the ability for people to express their cultural identities without fear of genocidal persecution.

In 1968, Chief Justice Warren expressed his regret at this state of affairs, saying, "We as a nation should have been the first to ratify the Genocide Convention....Instead, we may well be near the last...." (Address of Chief Justice Earl Warren before the National Conference on Continuing Action for Human Rights (Dec. 4, 1968), quoted from American Bar Association that the U. S. ratify the Convention on the Prevention and Punishment of the Crime of Genocide, 1969, at p.12.)

---

4. The Law for the Protection of German Blood and Honor. Sept. 15, 1935 (RGBL I. pp.1146-7).

5. Act. XVI, Hening Statutes, Vol. 3, pp.86-88.

6. Act 55 of 1949.

* Title taken from William Korey, "America's Shame: The Unratified Genocide Convention," Midstream, Vol. 27, No. 3 (1981), pp.7-13.

Now, in 1982, fourteen years on from Justice Warren's statement, the Convention remains unratified and America is even closer to "the last," other nations having ratified in the interim period. The controversy over U. S. ratification has a tortuous and complicated history. In the words of Lev E. Dobriansky, a colleague of the father of the convention, Raphael Lemkin, and a devoted worker towards U. S. ratification for over 30 years, "The story of this long ordeal consists of numerous ironies, unbelievable manipulations, fake argumentations, and even a personal tragedy." (Genocide, the Convention and Politics, Ukrainian Quarterly, 1978, 34(1): 39-39 at p.31.)

The objections in the early years were based on several factors. One was that genocide, along with human rights, is essentially a domestic concern and, therefore, does not meet the test of the Supreme Court as to whether the treaty is properly the subject of negotiations with a foreign country. Another argument was based on the federal character of the U. S. The claim was that ratification would create a constitutional issue by tilting the balance of authority on criminal matters between federal government and the states to the former. Another fear was that it would be used to attack the U. S. with regard to internal civil rights issues. Dobriansky summarizes the main objections in the Senate Hearings of the early years, saying: "Opponents of the Convention admixed it with civil rights, dangers to states rights, charges of genocide against negroes, an international plot against our form of government, and a whole assortment of sophistry as to the constitutional and legal perils of the treaty." (Lev. E. Dobriansky, Ukrainian Quarterly, 1970, 26 (3/4) 237-250 at p.237.)

The convention was not ratified by the Senate following the Sub-Committee Hearings in 1950; although they had reported favorably but had required that four "understandings" and a "declaration" be embodied in the resolution consenting to ratification. This was sufficient to prevent immediate ratification and a final committee vote on the issue was prevented by the Korean War and the growth of anti-communist feeling amongst right wing groups. "The Genocide Convention was perceived in these quarters as undermining American sovereignty and serving the interests of communism." ("America's Shame: The Unratified Genocide Treaty." William Korey, Midstream, 1981, 27(3):7-13 at p.10.)

Throughout the 1950's, opponents to ratification were vociferous: among these Senator John Bricker of Ohio, who was fearful of international intervention in American domestic affairs in that the treaty presented a threat to sovereignty, and the American Bar Association, too, was among the opponents.

The convention remained unratified throughout the 1960's when changes in attitudes amongst previous opponents began to emerge. In 1969, the American Bar Association's Section of Individual Rights and Responsibilities recommended ratification.

The dismissal of the many objections to ratification which the Section of Individual Rights and Responsibilities provides in its report merits

closer attention. It rejects the objection to the concept of government
action by treaties which caused so much alarm in the early 50's by pointing
to the thousands of international agreements into which the U. S. has entered since that time "without any noticeable diminuition of its sovereign
independence, nor any noticeable debasement of its standards to an international average." (Report of Section of Individual Rights and Responsibilities at p.20. Full Title supra. at p. .)

Secondly, the report rejects the contention that treaties, and particularly the Genocide Convention, undermine the force of Article 2(7) of the
U. N. Charter dealing with the matters "essentially within the domestic
jurisdiction of states." They reject this notion on the grounds that domestic matters remain outside the bounds of the United Nations, the Genocide
Convention simply covers a particular crime whatever the country in which
it is committed and involves all countries in a mutual responsibility to
punish the perpetrators.

Furthermore, the report rejects the argument that the Convention
might be used to justify federal legislation in the field of civil rights
and draws attention to the advances in civil rights legislation which have
taken place since 1949 as evidence that the U. S. Constitution provides
sufficient machinery to enable the passing of civil rights legislation
without any need for the authority of the Convention.

Despite the vehement rejection of these objections to ratification
offered by the Section of Individual Rights and Responsibilities, the ABA
House of Delegates itself remained firm on its stance of oppositon to
ratification. Further favorable action was taken by the Senate Foreign
Relations Committee in 1971 when they voted 10-4 in favor of ratification.

Then in 1976, the major turnaround took place, when the House of
delegates of the ABA finally voted for ratification. THE NEW YORK TIMES
commented on the decision in the following terms:

> "The turnabout by the ABA House of Delegates at its
> recent meeting in Philadelphia removes an aura of respect-
> ability in which opponents of the Convention—in the Senate
> and elsewhere—had been able to cloak themselves for more
> than a quarter century." (THE NEW YORK TIMES, "To Banish
> Genocide," February 26, 1976.)

Despite the retreat of its major opponents, however, in 1982 the
Convention remains unratified.

Lev. E. Dobiansky referred to a "personal tragedy along the road of
struggle towards ratification" (see p.). The victim of tragedy was
Raphael Lemkin, who gave birth to both the word "genocide" and the Convention, being a major contributor to the drafting process. Lemkin knew
of the horrors of genocide from personal experience: a member of a large
extended family in Poland, he lost 70 relatives in the Holocaust which
left himself and one brother as the only survivors. He devoted the

remainder of his life after 1948 to attempts to achieve U. S. ratification. When he died in 1959, his goal was still unobtained. As Dobriansky explains, Lemkin "spent his time and energies, and with increasing personal poverty, in the halls of the United Nations and our Capitol, promulgating this vital treaty. His death was premature. He died a sad and disillusioned man, not understanding how some had failed to understand the crucial import of the treaty. It was, above all, the United States, his adopted country, that he placed his complete faith in leadership on this."

The time has come to justify Lemkin's faith, to ratify a Convention which condemns a crime so abhorrent that its full manifestations almost defy belief. Let us, too justify the hope of those victims of the Holocaust whose faith in humanity remained steadfast despite their exposure to the worst kind of inhumanity. Let us fulfill their dream as expressed in the song of the Buchenwald inmates:

> O Buchenwald, we whimper not nor repine
> and no matter what our future should be
> we affirm life, we do not resign for
> the day is coming in which we shall be free

(Taken from: Bruno Apitz, "Nackt Unter Wolfen" (halle/Salle: Mitteldentscher Verlag, 1958) and quoted in The Annals of the American Academy of Political and Social Science, Vol. 450 July 1980, at p.19. From "Historical Antecedents: Why the Holocaust," by Claude R. Foster, Jr.)

Let us remember, also, that vital though ratification may be in order that the U. S. should join the many other nations who have already ratified, in stating publicly their commitment to condemnation and prevention of this abhorrent crime, as always "actions speak louder than words." Ratification must not be a mere moral gesture but a firm commitment to practical policies designed to immobilize regimes that are following the repulsive pattern of oppression and destruction which we have seen in periods of American and German history.

SIGNS OF OPPRESSION: PRE-NAZI GERMANY

PROFESSOR DEBORAH HERTZ

This semester I am teaching a large lecture class on the Holocaust. My students are largely Jewish, from the New York metropolitan
area. Many tend to have quite decided views, often without rich knowledge of facts. They very much tend to unabashedly view the Holocaust
through the sharp lenses of hindsight, with remarkably black-and-white
divisions of the historical actors into heroic Jewish victims and blood-
thirsty German murderers. That they think at all about the Holocaust
is a massive achievement which many in this room have worked hard to
accomplish. But as a scholar whose stock-in-trade is nuance, ambiguity,
and the battle to explain what is ugly and repugnant, my students' smug
and easy answers constantly trouble me. That my attempt to create grey
out of black and white also troubles some of them came very clear to me
when one of my teaching assistants reported on a conversation he had
overheard on a campus bus. He listened in as one student reported to
another her concern that I was "giving the Nazi side of the story."

Several weeks have passed since that conversation on the bus, and
I think that the passage of time has given my students more patience
with my approach to these matters. For the more that they themselves
begin to get tangled up in trying to account for why ordinary Germans
could become Eichmanns, or on the other side of the coin, why ordinary
Jews could join the Jewish Police, they too see more grey than they
did at the beginning of the semester. But I hardly think that my under-
graduates, who are, after all, bright and sensitive, are the only students of the Holocaust or of the Jewish or the German past who have
problems giving satisfying complex answers to the hardest question of
our century: how was Auschwitz possible?

What I want to do tonight is to suggest that insofar as historian
and non-historian alike look back into the history of the Jews in Germany
before January 30, 1933, the lenses of hindsight distort more than they
reveal. I think this problem has its origin in a common tendency to
assume, perhaps at a deep psychological level, that terrible events
must be the consequence of terrible, deep-seated, long-term causes or
precursors, that nothing as innovatively awful as the Holocaust could have
happened if relationships between Jews and gentiles had not been very
bad, indeed sick, for a very long time. Since it was Germany where
Nazism was born, came to power, and was the land out of which the Final
Solution was exported, there has been a powerful urge, almost a compul-
sion, to find especial fault with the history of Jewish-gentile relationships within Germany itself. It was little news that there was widespread,
frequently violent antisemitism in eastern Europe. But all accounts suggest that however convenient the Nazis found eastern European antisemitism
in the execution of their plans, eastern European antisemitism was quite

a different historical animal, one which had no direct role in causing Auschwitz. No, to uncover precursors one had to go shopping in the German past itself.

And precursors were indeed found. This search for precursors of Nazism in the German-Jewish past was itself a logical step for historians in the immediate post-war years, who reacted against a dominant tendency in O.S.S. (Office of Strategic Services) academic circles to explain Auschwitz as the demented creation of a relatively small group of demented Nazi leaders. So it was reasonable and useful to open up the historical canvas to include older centuries and long-dead people. Many of the books searching out precursors were written in the 1950s and early 1960s, at a time when intellectual history was the dominant genre of history-writing, and when the German past as a whole was being given a pretty tough beating. I do not want to be misunderstood here. Historical studies written in this style—notably the vast output of George Mosse—have made a crucial contribution to our knowledge of the German-Jewish past. By resurrecting obscure pamphlets and obscure thinkers, the "intellectual precursor" histories have helped us to fill in the links in the complex and changing chain of antisemitic thinking in Germany between Luther and Hitler.

But the very power of these books in making a connection between sixteenth-century thoughts and twentieth-century thoughts and events had as the other side of their coin decidedly deterministic assumptions about the continuity of antisemitic thought in Germany and the power of this ideological tradition in causing Auschwitz. Many passages, especially those in chapters of very general books on the Holocaust devoted to the "German-Jewish background," read as if Nazi antisemitism was, if you like organic metaphors, a seed in the ground just waiting for the right conditions to sprout. Or, if you prefer a sci-fi high-tech metaphor, as if these ideas travelled through German time in a sealed capsule, only to explode in 1933. Listen to the opening and closing words of a widely-used volume on the Holocaust, Lucy Dawidowicz's The War Against the Jews. She begins the chapter with: "A line of anti-Semistic descent from Martin Luther to Adolf Hitler is easy to draw," and ends it with "National Socialism was the consummation toward which the omnifacious anti-Semitic movements had striven for 150 years."(1)

It is important to remember that the precursor, continuity picture of the history of antisemitism had as its corollary a great deal of blaming, not just of antisemitic German thinkers, but of Jewish political actors as well. Historians' negative judgments about Jewish actions—or more to the point, their inactions—came quite quickly to the fore in works on the history of Zionism and Jewish self-defense in the period of the Second Reich, between 1871 and 1918. The tendency of Jewish notables to fear that self-defense against antisemitism would further incite antisemitism, their notion that full legal, political, and social integration was a privilege to be earned rather than a right to be demanded, indeed, the Jewish community's basic inability to keep its members from converting and marrying gentiles and to unite the warring internal Jewish factions have all been greeted with barely-hidden scorn and dismay by post-Holocaust Jewish historians. The implication is that if nineteenth-century Jews had been less enthusiastic about assimilation, none of the grisly events summed up by reference to Auschwitz could ever have happened.

It should be evident by this point that I (along with other members of a younger generation of historians of Germany) rather violently disagree with the idealist and deterministic assumptions of the precursor school. A hefty portion of our disagreement begins over the issue of method. The rapid rise and by now almost hegemonic place of social history as the queen of Clio's domain has led many of us to ponder long and hard before we assume that the creation of specific ideas in the first place, and the subsequent connections between ideas and events, is at all simple. Moreover, there is a new current in the writing of German history, specifically, which is challenging altogether the idea that German history in the nineteenth century was following a special or sick path compared to the path followed by English or French history. These new gadflies, a circle of English historians of Germany, have caused a stir in German academic circles by questioning whether economic and political progress in the "model" lands of England and France was as continuous and rapid as such progress has been assumed to have been, and whether pre-World War One Germany, in contrast, was as backward and reactionary as it has been taken to have been.(2)

I predict that all of these attacks on the post-war paradigm of German historiography will eventually result in a rewriting of the Jewish section of the German past as well. I hope that such a rewriting will restore to long-dead Jewish Germans the dignity of their position while they were alive, a dignity which I feel has all too often been stripped from them by historians who are driven to find in the past evil or sick precursors and causes for evil and tragic events. My own contribution to this rewriting will be my study of the Jewish literary salons which flourished in Berlin during the last two decades of the eighteenth century, at the time of the French Revolution. In this book (which was originally my dissertation) I show the enormous success a small group of wealthy Jewish women had as hostesses and as intellectual partners for the leading gentile writers and political figures of Berlin in these years. These Jewish salonières have often been blamed by Jewish historians because their social success as hostesses was frequently accompanied by conversion to Protestantism and intermarriage.

My analysis of the salonières' dilemma is quite different. My reading of the theological developments within Judaism itself during this era, as well as of the phenomenal welcome the salonières received from the cream of noble society in Berlin, suggest that the salonières' abandonment of their faith was a comparatively innocent, optimistic affair. The progress they had seen, indeed the progress they themselves had forged during their own lifetimes was good reason to believe that Judaism might well disappear in speedy historical time. If the ship was going to sink, why not jump off sooner rather than later, if conversion was a necessary precondition for obtaining noble husbands, social acceptance, university professorships, and a host of other goodies German society reserved only for gentiles, by birth or otherwise?

Now some of you, even without listening to more about my version of the story of the Jewish salons of eighteenth-century Berlin, may well be willing to be persuaded that I may indeed be right about the eighteenth century. Perhaps it is true that Jews then were innocent and optimistic when they triumphantly participated in German high culture. Maybe the modern period did begin on a good note—after all, this was the era of the Enlightenment—or maybe the salons were simply an exception in the degree of power they offered Jews in general and Jewish women in particular.

But the more I study the ensuing 150 years of Jewish life in Germany after salons, the more convinced I become that the search for precursors and the corollary blame heaped on Jewish leaders for their persistent hope that assimilation would work is also problematic for the later period A recent review of the diary of one of Carl Gustav Jung's patients, a woman caught up in the complexity of being Jewish in early twentieth-century central Europe, has boldly claimed that the only real choices facing Jews then and there were conversion or Zionism.(3) My argument is precisely the reverse. The reviewer and I agree, to be sure, that by the close of the nineteenth century, traditional, Orthodox Judaism was not a realistic choice for most of the Jewish Germans, who were by and large educated professionals. And although conversion was an important alternative for ever-increasing numbers of Jews in Germany, since the days of the late eighteenth century, its meaning had changed, and con-version had gradually come to reek of opportunism, of bad faith. Memoirs and biographies tell us very emphatically that many prominent Jews re-fused to convert, not because they believed in any substantive Jewish faith, but because they did not want to sell out, as it were, so conver-sion was problematic. As for Zionism, it had difficulties in attract-ing many Jews, precisely because of their own success in Germany.

I would maintain that the middle, assimilationist road, the ambigu-ous, difficult attempt to somehow remain Jewish yet also continue to become more "German" was a viable strategy well up to the closing days of 1932. The explicitly antisemitic parties which sprang up during and after the depression of the 1870s had faded away by the first decade of the twentieth century. To be sure, racial antisemitism was widely legiti-mized even by the temporary success of these parties and by the new popu-larity of their platform in academic circles. But the pre-1914 Conserva-tive Party, heir to the ideology of the defunct antisemitic parties, was by no means consistent in its advocacy of antisemitism.

But surely, many here would remind me, nothing more was up for grabs after World War One. Surely then the assimilationist point of view was "false consciousness." I will admit that the question of how clear the Nazi program was in the twenties about Nazi plans to "solve" the Jewish problem is still hotly debated. But I would also stress that there is plenty of evidence before 1933 to suggest that the Nazi party might well hold together its supporters without extensive reliance on antisemitism. As is there evidence even after 1933 that gentile anti-semitism in Germany might well be too latent, indeed too mild, for the Nazis to employ it successfully to glue together their disparate classes of supporters.

My point is that when studying the Holocaust, we must not cheapen and degrade its victims, and the task of explanation, by reading the past backwards. It happened forwards, day by day, and intelligent Jews then disagreed about what might happen, and consequently, about what they should do. In sum, I do not think the well-informed historical traveller poking around in the German past before 1933 will find only, or even predominantly, overt signs of religious or racial oppression. On the contrary, such a time traveller is likely to find phenomenal economic and cultural success, and slow but real political progress. Some signs of Jewish oppression in Germany before 1933 were there, to be sure, but they were more likely to be the subtle and personal com-plexities which often accompany the partial and incomplete integration of a privileged, by no means an outcast minority. Indeed, it was the very incompleteness of Jewish integration which fueled Jewish cultural creativity. It was decades of Jewish success at the top of society, rather than Jewish failure at its bottom, which allowed the Nazi leader-ship to eventually harness the antisemitism which did exist in Germany to mask the splits in their coalition, and allow Hitler to have his final, evil solution to what was primarily his own, and not his people's problem.

It is not that Jewish-gentile relationships in Germany before 1933 were universally perfect or that they are irrelevant in uncovering the causes for Auschwitz. My plea is only the modest one that they were complex relationships with a complex relationship to the short-term logic and illogic which caused Auschwitz. German Jewry was not allowed to continue its grand and intelligent civilization. Let us, as we study them and their creations, not rob them of their glory and of their opti-mism that things might have turned out very differently indeed.

NOTES

1. Lucy Dawidowicz, The War Against the Jews (New York, 1975), 29 and 62.

2. The gadflies are David Blackbourn and Geoff Eley, and their attack is Mythen deutcher Geschichtsschreibung (Frankfurt/M., 1980).

3. Melvyn Hill, "Women, Jews, and Madness," Village Voice Literary Supplement 11 (October, 1982).

REFLECTIONS ON UNEMPLOYMENT, GENOCIDE AND BUREAUCRACY

RICHARD L. RUBENSTEIN

With unemployment rising to its highest levels since the Great Depression in both the United States and Europe, it is once again painfully apparent that few problems confronting modern civilization have been as insidiously corrupting or as destructive of the common good as the phenomenon of mass surplus population.

In 1933 in the midst of the Great Depression, poet Allen Tate offered his own solution to the problem of unemployment, the gassing of the unemployed and their families:

> ...unless we deal with the permanently unemployed, we shall have trouble. The masses of the unemployed are not consuming. They are beginning to engage in anti-social pursuits...and in twenty years...this class may increase to fifty million men. If the number increases or its even allowed to remain constant, it will...constitute a dire menace to public order...Society would suffer the least rupture....if it quietly and in the ordinary routine of industrial technology, killed off about eight million workers and their families.
>
> It should be done, all things considered, gradually, but completed in a year lest there should be an abnormal increase of that class of persons, with the attendant perils...
>
> I need not suggest that the method be painless. We are too humane for the axe, guillotine, rope or firing squad. I should personally prefer some kind of lethal gas, but not being a chemist, I leave that proposal to the specialists...
>
> I have said that this method of disposing of the residue X would relieve us of the whole problem of unemployment. That is not strictly true. It assumes as accomplished a long moratorium on the invention of labour-elimination devices; it requires for its success a stabilization of our technology. Yet should our technical equipment still further improve, the method is still workable. There would merely be a certain number of newly unemployed to kill off every year.(1)

Tate's article was entitled "The Problem of the Unemployed: A Modest Proposal" and was reminiscent of Jonathan Swift's "Modest Proposal." As is well known, Swift's solution to the problem of redundant poor children in his time was simple: fatten them and eat them. The proposals of both Swift and Tate are examples of black humor, but, they have their serious side. One of the functions of black humor is to permit the expression of morally repugnant ideas in a form that disguises their fundamental seriousness. Regretably, what is black humor in a period of relative stability could become a real temptation in a period of chronic instability. As every child of this century knows, it is possible to "solve" the problem of surplus people by outright extermination. At present we are nowhere near that point. Nevertheless, we would be well advised to recognize the wisdom behind the intuition of a distinguished American poet. As he understood years before World War II, mass unemployment and genocide are related phenomena. Genocide is the most radical means available to public authorities to dispose of an unwanted population. We should, however, note that, unlike irrational mob violence, for its successful implementation a genocide requires rational, impersonal, routinized, and value-neutral institutions of social organization capable of effectively and economically identifying, disarming, collecting, and disposing of the target population.(2) Bureaucratic organization is required by the very size of the target population.

Before proceeding, I would like to suggest that our effort to understand genocide will be materially enhanced if we regard the phenomenon as the most radical type of state-sponsored program of population elimination. Such a program is one in which the state's decision-makers target for removal a sector of the population under its control. Among who have been so targeted are members of deviant nationalities or religious communities, redundant economic and social classes, unreconciled political opponents, and defeated enemy populations. All population elimination programs have a common aim. They do, however, differ in the means employed. Relatively mild methods include emigration and colonization schemes. Harsher methods include legal discrimination and physical harassment designed to encourage emigration, compulsory segregation of the target population in specialized containment precincts (such as the Poor House in England, the urban ghetto, and the modern concentration camp), abusive institutions of compulsory, involuntary servitude (e.g. the Soviet Gulags), and enforced expulsion. As noted, extermination is the most radical but by no means the only method of population elimination.

It would be comforting to think that all such programs are only of historical interest. Unfortunately, they may not be. Indeed, we may be in the midst of the latter stages of a long-range historical crisis rooted in the simple fact that by producing a surplus, men take the first step in making themselves superfluous.

In the past, migration alleviated the problem of surplus people. The fortunate availability of the New World gave Europe's surplus the promise of a new beginning. From 1740 to 1914 the total number of people of European stock increased from about 120,000,000 to 718,000,000. As Europe industrialized, out-migration accelerated. Thus, between 1875 and 1880 there was an average annual emigration of 280,000 persons; between 1880 and 1885 the figure was 685,000; between 1885 and 1890 the annual average was 730,000. In the peak year of 1910, 2,000,000 left Europe!

Any civilization that loses as many people as did Europe between the end of the Napoleonic Wars and the beginning of World War I is a civilization in crisis. However, the crisis was somewhat disguised by the fact that there were vast areas available for European settlement and people of European origin enjoyed an absolute technological superiority over non-European peoples until the beginning of the twentieth century. This enabled the Europe's surplus human beings: (a) to expand over very large areas of the earth with minimal resistance from the indigenous populations; (b) exploitatively to dominate most non-European peoples, utilizing their labor and natural resources under conditions extremely favorable to the Europeans; (c) to create and maintain an industrial and technological civilization in which most of the non-European peoples were customers rather than competitors. These conditions permitted a far greater expansion of the economies of the European peoples than would have been the case had all of the peoples of the world entered the technological age simultaneously. Europe's technological headstart also permitted the absorption of more Europeans in the work force than would otherwise have been the case. Nevertheless, in spite of the never-to-be repeated advantages enjoyed by the European peoples, Europe was unable to escape the extraordinary social dislocations of two world wars, the Russian Revolution, the Spanish Civil War, Fascism, and National Socialism.

Unfortunately, the problem of population redundancy that plagued industrializing Europe for so long is now plaguing most of the developing and developed nations alike. Moreover, the world today is vastly different from what it was even a decade ago. The peoples of European origin are no longer technologically superior to non-Europeans, especially the peoples of the Orient. In addition to Japan, South Korea, Taiwan, Singapore, and Hong Kong have demonstrated a phenomenal capacity to compete with the West in developing a type of civilization originally endogenic to the West and exogenic to Asia. (3) This is a fact of awesome significance for the future of the world, especially when one considers the long-range economic and technological potentialities of the People's Republic of China.

Whatever the outcome of the ongoing technological transformation of Asia, it is obvious that societies of European origin can no longer solve the problem of surplus people by exporting it. This was understood by Adolf Hitler. As we know, his "solution" included genocide and wars of enslavement and extermination. Moreover, if genocide is seen as the most radical state-sponsored program of population elimination, it becomes apparent that the National Socialist program of genocide was the culmination of a lengthy development having its origins in the first European attempts at modernization. Put differently, the rise of surplus peoples has almost always been an unintended consequence of the ongoing rationalization of the economy and society which has characterized first European and then world history since the end of the Middle Ages.

The enclosure movement in England can be seen as one of the earliest population elimination programs of the modern period. The Acts of Enclosure were a series of legal and political measures enacted from the sixteenth to the nineteenth centuries that had the effect of consolidating uneconomical small agrarian holdings by evicting peasants from their ancient domiciles and thereby creating the basis for capitalist agriculture. By destroying the customary rights of the lower stratum of the English peasantry, the enclosures facilitated the transformation of the peasants into a landless agricultural and industrial proletariat. Because many of the evicted peasants were unable to find work, the enclosure movement also resulted in mass unemployment in the first country to modernize its agriculture. As we shall see, there is a thread of continuity linking the English program of population elimination that deprived hundreds of thousands, if not millions, of peasants of their homes and the more radical state-sponsored programs of population elimination of the twentieth-century which have successfully removed target populations numbering millions from the human world altogether.

Still, the story has two sides. The enclosures have been defended by both conservative and Marxists writers on English land policy. According to Barrington Moore, Jr., the enclosures were a necessary form of "revolutionary violence" that made English democracy possible through the "final solution of the peasant question," a phrase uncomfortably reminiscent of Reinhardt Heydrich's announcement on January 20, 1942 that the Fuhrer had decided upon the "final solution of the Jewish question" (4) Nevertheless, even those who find Moore's language problematic tend to agree that the enclosures did lay the foundation for the modernization of British agriculture.

In all likelihood, the tradition-bound peasants would have eventually lost their holdings even if there had been no official action. In a subsistence economy with a rapidly growing population, either some people leave the land in every generation or the land will eventually be subdivided beyond the point at which it can sustain small cultivators, as indeed happened in Ireland and elsewhere at a later time. In any event, peasants committed to subsistence farming stood in the way of "progress" and were brutally swept away. They had become an economically and socially redundant class and suffered the bitter consequences of their superfluity.

Those dispossessed English peasants who could find no work, and there were many, became the vanguard of all of the ensuing displaced rural populations that were to be confronted with mass unemployment and were to become dependent on welfare and deviant economic activity, including crime, to stay alive. As R. H. Tawney has observed, although poverty was hardly new, the phenomenon of large numbers of willing, able-bodied men who could find no work was without precedent. (5) The magnitude of the problem can be seen in the fact that in 1688 it was estimated that there were no fewer than 60,000 vagrant families in England or approximately 300,000 people out of a total population of about 5,500,000.(6)

The state could not ignore the thousands who had been set adrift. From the sixteenth century onward, a system of poor relief was developed in response to the growing numbers of dependent paupers. The poor laws were both welfare and police measures. As is the case today, the poor had to be fed; they also had to be controlled. Although a Christian spirit originally motivated the system of almsgiving and often acted as a break against the worst abuses, there is little disagreement that there were often disgraceful abuses in the treatment of paupers. We need not detail that treatment in this context save to note one instructive incident at a later stage in the evolution of the system. In 1935 an Assistant Poor Law Commissioner reported that in parts of England the poor refused to accept food offered them, believing it had been poisoned in order to kill them off. They also believed that when the children in a pauper family exceeded three in number the excess was to be killed off, and all young children and women under eighteen were to be sterilized.(7)

The worst fears of the poor appeared to be confirmed by the appearance in 1838 of a number of works originally written for private circulation advocating the extermination of superfluous pauper infants. The actual authorship of these works has never been ascertained. Nevertheless, the fears of the poor cannot be dismissed as simple paranoia. The poor could not fail to understand their own superfluity or the options available to the state in dealing with them. (8)

Not surprisingly, as the system was professionalized, it tended to become progressively dehumanized. It is fair to say that the dehumanization reached its worst with the passage of the Poor Law Reform of 1834. The person most responsible for the 1834 Report of the Poor Law Commission was Sir Edwin Chadwick. Chadwick was a disciple of Jeremy Bentham. His approach to the care of the Indigent was based upon Bentham's principle of "less eligibility," namely, "...that the condition of the person relieved at public expense must be made less eligible on the whole than the person living on the fruits of his own labour."(9) Both Bentham and Chadwick regarded the "less eligibility" principle as an infallible guarantee that public funds would not be expended on any but the indubitably indigent. In practical terms, Chadwick designed a system in which the conditions under which poor relief was distributed to able-bodied men were so utterly degrading that only the most desperate applied. In order to receive public assistance, a pauper had to commit himself and his family to the poor house where the sexes were separated, families broken up, and the laxer routines of the poor gave way to the deliberately calculated and rationalized terror of a depersonalized regimen. In many ways, the English poor house of the nineteenth century anticipates the concentration camps of the twentieth century. Both institutions had as their purpose the isolation, segregation and exploitation of a target population which could not be incarcerated through normal judicial procedures but which the state attempted to remove from normal contact with the larger society. (10)

Even harsh and ungenerous welfare constitutes a relatively humane way of dealing with a surplus population in comparison with the methods that were to follow. "Poor relief" controlled the indigent and segregated them from the rest of the population, but it did not altogether eliminate them from their native communities as did the population-elimination policies that were to follow.

The period between 1760 and 1844 witnessed the greatest number of acres enclosed and families evicted. The Irish famine was at its worst between 1846 and 1848. It was the misfortune of famine-struck Ireland that the fate of its peasants was in the hands of the same English government that was so harshly indifferent to the fate of its own peasants. The Irish famine of 1846 to 1848 was one of the greatest demographic catastrophes of the nineteenth century. Out of a population conservatively estimated at 9,000,000, Ireland lost approximately 2,500,000 people, half of whom emigrated and half perished. As a result of the famine, the Irish lost a greater proportion of their population than did any other community in modern times, save the Jews, the Armenians and, more recently, the Kampucheans.

When the failure of the potato crop became known, many of Ireland's absentee British landlords were eager to get rid of tenants whom they knew would be unable to pay the rent. As in the case of the enclosures, there was money to be made by eliminating uneconomical subsistence producers and replacing them with farmers or sheepraisers who could produce a cash crop. There was, however, an important difference between the two countries. In England, eviction resulted in throwing dispossessed peasants on poor relief; in Ireland eviction could be tantamount to a death sentence especially in the midst of famine. Merciless mass evictions were one of the worst aspects of the famine. Starving, impoverished peasants were turned out of their holdings and their cabins immediately torn down, often in the harshest winter weather. Instead of declaring a moratorium on debts or offering some kind of disaster relief, the English government employed its troops to drive away hunger-weakened families.

As the crisis worsened, Charles Edward Trevelyan, England's Assistant Secretary of the Treasury and the ultimate arbiter of all public funds spent on Irish relief, called a halt to almost all public relief programs at a time when Ireland's need for help was most urgent. Trevelyan never went as far as Nassau W. Senior, the famous political economist and Chadwick's partner in formulating the Poor Law Reform of 1834, who expressed regret that the famine had killed only one million people, but he did express the opinion that the mass deaths were the unanticipated way an "all-wise Providence" had solved the problem of Ireland's imbalance between population and food.(11) Trevelyan also wrote of his satisfaction at the large numbers of peasants who were forced to emigrate because of the famine:

> I do not know how farms are to be consolidated if
> small farmers do not emigrate and by acting for
> the purpose of keeping them at home, we should be
> defeating our own object. We must not complain of
> what we really want to obtain. If small farms go,
> and then landlords are induced to sell portions of
> their estates to persons who will invest capital,
> we shall at last arrive at something like a satis-
> factory settlement in this country.(12)

There was, of course, another way to clear Ireland of "small farmers" and make way for "persons who will invest capital": do nothing during the famine and let the unwanted people die. Trevelyan based his policy on the conviction that the famine could best be dealt with by leaving matters to "the operation of natural causes." Trevelyan was wholly supported by the Prime Minister, Lord John Russell, who in 1848 refused to consider granting of further public funds to assist Ireland.

While Trevelyan would never have done anything to kill the Irish outright, as Hitler caused the Jews to be killed a century later, he was committed to a policy which had the effect of condemning them to death. If this was not apparent to Trevelyan, who was regarded as a highly competent bureaucrat and is credited with having been the creator of England's modern civil service system, it was to Twistleton, the Poor Law Commissioner for Ireland who finally resigned, declaring that he considered himself to be an "unfit agent for a policy which must be one of extermination."(13) A similar observation was made by Lord Clarendon, the Lord Lieutenant of Ireland, in a letter to the Prime Minister. Commenting on the indifference of the British Parliament to Irish suffering, Clarendon wrote:

> "...I don't think there is another legislature in
> Europe that would disregard such sufferings as now
> exist in the West of Ireland, or coldly persist in
> a policy of extermination."(14)

Incidentally, the Irish emigrants can be seen as the first modern "boat people." In at least one respect, English policy resembled Hanoi's. Both governments were concerned with encouraging the departure of a target population deemed undesirable; neither government was concerned with their safe passage elsewhere. It is, for example, authoritatively estimated that of the 100,000 Irish emigrants who left for North America in 1847, approximately 38,000 perished, 17,000 at sea and the remainder from disease after they landed. Conditions on many of the emigrant ships were so bad that they were known as "coffin ships."

Modernization of Irish agriculture was not the only reason Britain welcomed what an editorial writer in THE ECONOMIST called "the departure of the redundant part of the population of Ireland." (15) Ireland's population was increasing at twice the rate of England's. Because of their extreme poverty, the Irish were willing to work in the industrial towns of England, sometimes as strikebreakers, at lower wages than those British and Scottish workers would accept. The Irish were both a necessary component in the industrial expansion of England and a destabilizing element. One did not have to be a Malthusian to see that there was an upper limit to Irish emigration, just as there may be a limit to immigration to the United States today.

Ireland's population increase was also a potential military threat. England had little reason to fear Ireland directly. Nevertheless, in any war England could be certain that Ireland's heart would be with England's enemies. The weaker and the less numerous were the Irish, the less likely they would ever become a serious threat to England's security.

In this respect, English apprehensions concerning the Irish were not unlike those of Turkey concerning the Armenians at the beginning of the twentieth century. The Turks had little reason for confidence in the loyalty of the Christian Armenians, whose homeland straddled both sides of the frontier between Moslem Turkey and Christian Russia. Although the overt behavior of the Armenians gave the Turks little warrant for action against them, they were regarded as an objective danger by the modernizing Young Turks who had overthrown the corrupt and backward regime of Sultan Abdul Hamid in 1908. When in 1915 wartime conditions made possible resort to radical measures, the Turkish government instituted a thoroughly modern, bureaucratically organized, systematic program of genocide against its Armenian citizens. (16)

Unlike the Turkish government, the British government did not inaugurate an active program of genocide against an unreconciled border people. It did, however, "let nature take its course." No other action was necessary.

There may also be parallels between the course of action taken by the British government toward the Irish during the Irish famine and its conduct toward Europe's Jews during World War II. Possessing accurate knowledge of the Nazi program of extermination, the British government barred wartime Jewish immigration to Palestine. Moreover, the British Navy forced thousands of desperate Jewish "boat people" attempting to reach Palestine to return to certain death in Europe.

In the nineteenth century, England was a direct beneficiary of Ireland's tragedy. In the twentieth century, it was a beneficiary

of the extermination of the Jews. The smaller the number of Jews
who survived the war, the less urgent would be Jewish pressure on
Britain for immigration into Palestine. Apart from the action of
the British Navy in turning back the Jews, all that was necessary
for the British to eliminate yet another troublesome population
was to let "nature," in the form of the SS, take its course. If
the British government did not actively exterminate populations
it deemed undesirable, over a period of several centuries it pursued
policies that facilitated their elimination by one means or another.

Of all the state-sponsored population-elimination programs of
modern times, none came as close to destroying the entire target
population as the destruction of the European Jews. However,
Czarist Russia, not National Socialist Germany, appears to have
been the first modern state to attempt to eliminate the Jews from
its midst. With the doleful wisdom of hindsight, 1881 can be seen
as the watershed year in which the tragic fate of European Jewry
began to unfold. In that year pogroms broke out throughout much
of the Czarist empire. If the pogroms were not initiated by the
government, they were certainly tolerated by it.

The ultimate aim of Russian policy in the aftermath of the
pogroms of 1881 was the total elimination of the Jews. This was
clearly understood by one of the leaders most responsible for that
policy, Konstantin Petrovich Pobedonostsev (1827-1904), a highly
influential bureaucrat who served as "Supreme Prosecutor of the
Holy Synod" from 1880 until his death. Before assuming that office
he served as Professor of Civil Law at Moscow University (1860-65)
and tutor to Grand Duke Alexander (1865-81). The Grand Duke became
Tsar Alexander III in 1881. Historian James Billington has described
Pobedonostsev in a way that is reminiscent of another bureaucrat we
have met, Sir Charles Edward Trevelyan:

> Pobedonostsev...was a thoroughly prosaic lay figure,
> whose ideal was the gray efficiency and uniformity
> of the modern organization man. He was the prophet
> of duty, work, and order-shifting his bishops around
> periodically to prevent any distracting local attach-
> ments from impeding the smooth functioning of the
> ecclesiastical machine. He was unemotional, even
> cynical, about his methods. But they were generally
> effective and earn him a deserved place as one of the
> builders of the modern bureaucratic state.(17)

As a figure of consequence in Jewish history, Pobedonostsev is
perhaps best remembered for his own "solution" of the Jewish problem,
which he is reported to have offered a group of Jewish petitioners in
1898: "One third will die, one third will leave the country, and the
last third will be completely assimilated within the surrounding population."(18)

The pogroms of 1881 and thereafter had the desired effect. Within a decade, Jewish emigration from eastern Europe increased ten-fold. The goal of the anti-Semitic elements within the Czarist government was exactly the same as that of the National Socialists, namely, the elimination of the Jewish presence within their society. Admittedly, the means employed by the Czarist government, such as pogroms and official discrimination, seem "old fashioned" when compared to Hitler's. Nevertheless, the Czarist measures constituted one of the most effective state-sponsored programs of population elimination up to its time. They set in motion the mass emigration from eastern Europe of more than 4,000,000 Jews from 1881 to 1930. Never before had so many Jews migrated from one country to another in so short a time.

As the Jewish situation in eastern Europe became increasingly untenable, Jews migrated first to the urban centers of Germany and Austria. In 1846, 3,739 Jews lived in Vienna; in 1900 there were 176,000. In 1852, 11,840 Jews resided in Berlin. In 1890 there were 108,044. Unfortunately, as the eastern European Jews were entering Germany and Austria, Germany was experiencing the largest emigration in its history. Between 1871 and 1885, 1,678,202 people, approximately 3.5 percent of the entire population, migrated to the United States. The peak emigration occurred in the crucial year of 1881-1882.(19)

Moreover, as Germany industrialized, it experienced periods of mass unemployment. In 1891, ten years after the beginning of the decisive Russian pogroms, Leo von Caprivi, the Chancellor of the German Reich, observed that "Germany must export goods or people."(20) Like contemporary Japan, Germany's ability to produce exceeded her capacity to consume. Without foreign markets, Germany would be faced with an unacceptable level of mass unemployment at home. In Caprivi's time, emigration was considered the normal acceptable method of population elimination in Germany as well as elsewhere in Europe. It is estimated that in the nineteenth and early twentieth centuries 6,000,000 people emigrated from Germany and 5,200,000 from Austria-Hungary.(21)

Even as a young man in Vienna, Hitler was keenly interested in the phenomenon of German emigration. According to historian Robert G. L. Waite, one of the books in Hitler's library whose marginal notes attest the young Hitler's strong interest was Auswanderungs-Moglich-keiten in Argentinien (Emigration Possibilities in Argentina).(22) In Mein Kampf, Hitler wrote of the need for land to the east to absorb Germany's population surplus. He came to regard emigration to the New World as a poor solution to Germany's population problem for the emigrants ceased to be a human resource for Germany. Hitler's program of seeking Lebensraum in the east was designed to provide an area adjacent to the Reich to which Germany's surplus population could migrate. The demographic strength of the migrants would thus be retained by their native land.

Moreover, the young Hitler favored a rational, systematic,

bureaucratically organized program for the elimination of the Jews as
is evident from his letter of September 16, 1919, to Staff-Captain
Karl Mayr in which he discusses the difference between the "rational
grounds":

> Anti-Semitism on purely emotional grounds will find
> its ultimate expression in the form of pogroms. The
> anti-Semitism of reason (rational anti-Semitism) how-
> ever, must lead to a systematic and legal struggle
> against, and eradication of, what privileges the Jews
> now enjoy over other foreigners...Its final objective,
> however, must be the total removal (Entfernung) of all
> Jews from our midst."(23)

Thus, in his earliest political document Hitler revealed himself as a
thoroughly modern figure who had little faith in the efficacy of pogroms
and looked forward to a deliberately calculated, systematic policy for
the elimination of the Jews.

Many of the Nazi leaders, Hitler included, understood the urgency
of the problem of population redundancy through their own personal
experience. According to the German historian, Karl Dietrich Bracher,
before the seizure of power in 1933, most members of the Nazi inner
circles had been "petty bourgeois who had been for some time already
engaged in the futile pursuit of a career."(24) Nowhere is this more
evident than in the career of Hitler himself. Had he not succeeded in
making a career out of politics, he might have spent his life as a
shiftless outsider untrained for any normal vocation. Having escaped
redundancy by the success of their political movement, the National
Socialist elite was determined to bring the overseas Auswanderung to a
halt and redirect the flow of people eastward. Genocide was the almost
inevitable consequence of the National Socialist program of Lebensraum
and anti-Semitism as soon as wartime conditions gave the German government a free hand.

A little discussed, but important motive for the destruction of
the Jews of eastern Europe was to close off all possibility of their
immigration to Germany. By virtue of their numbers and their language,
the Jews of eastern Europe constituted an immense reservoir of potential
immigrants who might settle in Germany and Austria and compete with
members of the indigenous population. This apprehension was given expression even before the twentieth century. In 1879 historian Heinrich
von Treitschke complained that "year after year there pours a host of
ambitious pants-selling youngsters, whose children will some day control
...the stock exchanges and the newspapers."(25) In some ways it was
easier for eastern European Jews to adjust to German commercial and
cultural life than it was for Slavs. Eastern European Jews spoke a
German dialect, Yiddish. No other eastern European language was as
close to Yiddish as German. Incidentally, in 1982 fifteen West German
professors publicly expressed concern about the long range damage that

might be done to the quality of German cultural life by another group
of immigrants perceived to be unassimilable, namely, the Turkish Gastar-
beiter.

When the Germans invaded eastern Europe, they had a very simple
and demonically successful way of shutting off all future Jewish immigration, mass murder. This may explain why Himmler insisted on exterminat-
ing even those skilled Jewish laborers whom the Wehrmacht sought to
keep working in Polish war industries. Thus, even when the war was
lost, it was possible to achieve at least one crucial objective of
National Socialism, the elimination of the huge reservoir of eastern
European Jews whom the Germans feared might someday attempt to settle
in their land.(26)

The destruction of Europe's Jews was by no means the last state-
sponsored program of population elimination. We may be witnessing the
beginnings of such a program in Lebanon in the aftermath of the 1982
war. The Lebanese are apparently pursuing their own population-
elimination program. By means of pogroms and harassment, they are
apparently seeking to encourage the departure of Lebanon's unwanted
Palestinian community.

Among the most extensive elimination programs were the two that
took place in Indo-China in the aftermath of the Vietnamese war.
Within a few weeks of the fall of Phnom Penh on April 17, 1975,
Kampuchea's urban population was dumped into the jungles and country-
side without even rudimentary provisions. In addition, whole groups
were executed immediately. The Vietnamese estimate that 3,000,000
died out of a total Kampucheon population of 7,000,000. The American
estimate is 2,000,000.

Hanoi's program of population elimination was slower in coming.
When the South Vietnamese government collapsed and American spending
was terminated, approximately 3,000,000 people suddenly found themselves unemployed and, unless retrained, unemployable. Simply finding work for Vietnam's growing population was an insuperable task.
In 1950 the population was around 26,000,000. By 1975 it had grown
to at least 44,000,000.(27) The labor force was estimated to be
22,000,000 and was growing at a rate of some 1,000,000 a year!

Given Hanoi's commitment to communism, a commitment fortified by
years of war and victory over the world's leading capitalist power,
there was little reason to doubt the bourgeois and professional
classes of South Vietnam were targetted for elimination. Only the
means were uncertain. Moreover, ethnic conflict exacerbated class
conflict. A very large proportion of the commercial and professional
class were not Vietnamese but ethnic Chinese, called the Hoa in Vietnam.
Ethnic hostility between the Chinese and the Vietnamese has a long
history. During the war, it was in the interest of both Hanoi and
Saigon to mute the ethnic conflict. With Hanoi's victory, the situation

of the Hoa rapidly deteriorated. The Hoa were both an envied minority and a predominant element in the very class a communist government would seek to eliminate.

Systematic expulsion of Vietnam's Chinese minority seems to have begun in earnest in the wake of the Chinese invasion of February and March 1979. Hanoi's leadership seems to have decided that no Chinese could be trusted and that in one way or another, Vietnam had to eliminate them. The political leadership in Hanoi also decided to encourage the departure of those ethnic Vietnamese who were deemed unassimilable to the new society by reason of their economic or political background.

We cannot recount the terrible story of the Indo-Chinese refugees in this context, save to note that between 1975 and 1981, 1,014,596 refugees were resettled with the United States receiving 480,912. Yet, the more one reflects on the agony of Vietnam, the more one is likely to see all of the actors as trapped by a political, social and economic tragedy of oceanic proportions. After the war, most members of South Vietnam's middle class were faced with almost certain downward social mobility regardless of what economic system carried the day. Under Communism the middle class is being ruined by the state's economic policies. Under capitalism a market economy would have produced a roughly comparable result. Without a quantum leap in productivity, it was impossible for so large a number of people to enjoy the same status and amenities they did during the war. Moreover, there is little reason to believe that had Vietnam been unified by a capitalist govern- ment after thirty years of war, the ethnic Chinese would have fared much better than they have under Hanoi. History and geography had condemned the Vietnamese to perennial distrust, if not outright hostility, toward the Chinese. With rampant unemployment and a rapidly increasing labor force, the country was ripe for a natural or a man-made demographic catastrophe. Kampuchea was condemned to experience both. Vietnam's catastrophe was largely man-made. Nor can it be said that the crisis has yet come to an end. Amid the extra- ordinary prosperity of Vietnam's Asian neighbors, the fundamental economic and social problems that led to the mass expulsions in Vietnam itself have yet to be solved.

At the height of the refugee crisis, the elimination of the ethnic Chinese by Hanoi was frequently likened to the Nazi extermination of the Jews. Surely there are similarities, but there was a major dif- ference: while Hanoi was indifferent to the fate of the refugees, mass murder was not Hanoi's preferred method of population elimination. Un- fortunately, even this crucial difference might not hold in a future crisis. The absorptive capacities of the world's receiving nations is strictly limited. One of the nightmares facing the receiving nations is that the flow of refugees could overwhelm their absorptive capacities. This may have already happened in Thailand where the government is cur- rently insisting that all Kampuchean refugees must somehow depart in spite of the fact that few of the refugees can find a country willing

to accept them and there is little likelihood that those who return
to Kampuchea will survive. In view of the number of actual and
potential refugees in an overpopulated and underemployed world, the
possibility of more such nightmares will haunt humanity for the fore-
seeable future. As terrible as was the expulsion of the Hoa from
Indochina, the majority did escape with their lives and, albeit with
much difficulty, they were eventually permitted to settle elsewhere.
The same cannot be said of Europe's Jews. This observation is not
offered in defense of Hanoi's policies but as a caveat against over-
simplifying a monumental human tragedy.

When we turn from historical reflection to a consideration of
the current situation, it would appear that the policies of the Reagan
administration have intensified rather than ameliorated the crisis
of surplus people. This is, for example, evident in the administration's continuing attempts to curtail federal support for higher
education. In 1981-1982 an estimated 11,000,000 students were en-
rolled in American institutions of higher learning. In addition to
serving as training and certifying institutions, colleges and universities provide an appropriate environment in which unemployable young
people can wait their turn to enter the job market. Increasingly, the
higher-education system fulfills the same function for older people.
Recently, the number of "returnees" and "retreads" in America's
colleges and universities has increased greatly. In 1978, 1,500,000
Americans returned to colleges and universities for a second try at
higher education. Currently, more than one third of all post secondary
school students are 25 years old or older.(28) Without its distinctive
system of higher education, with its mass student population, America's
unemployment rate would be materially higher than it is now. So, too,
would be the level of middle-class resentment.

The seriousness of cutting federal support for higher education,
becomes especially apparent when one considers the potential impact
of the microelectronic revolution on the American economy in the
decades ahead. As we have seen in the past, almost all advances in
the rationalization of production have resulted in large-scale human
redundancies. Admittedly, the labor market has eventually absorbed
a very respectable segment of the available work force, but not before
monumental social dislocations intervened. With the advent of microcomputer robotics, we are on the threshold of a series of quantum
leaps in office and factory rationalization, and there is a high prob-
ability that we will experience social dislocations of unprecedented
magnitude. According to Business Week magazine, 45 percent of all of
the jobs in the labor force, almost 45,000,000, could be affected by
automotation during the next twenty years.(29) A large proportion of
the work force may find the jobs for which they were trained no longer
exist when they are in mid-career. Many workers will have to return
to school for further job training or even for training leading to a
meaningful alternative to a job. The long-term costs of controlling
angry and frustrated people whose jobs cease to exist could prove far

more expensive to society than subsidies permitting them to return to
school.

In addition to automation, changing patterns of government spending
and private investment are dramatically altering employment opportunities.
As a result of increased defense spending, demand for scientists, engi-
neers, and other skilled professionals is rising. Unfortunately, high-
technology defense production requires far fewer workers than do those
sectors of the economy which have felt the brunt of the restrictive
side of the administration's fiscal policies. During the nineteen-
seventies, the United States experienced an unprecedented growth in
employment. From 1973 to 1979, almost 13,000,000 new non-agricultural
jobs were created, 11,000,000 in the private sector. Seventy percent
of the new jobs were in retail trade and in service occupations.(30)
Most of the jobs were low-paying with scant opportunity for advancement.
Nevertheless, millions of Americans preferred even dead-end jobs to
dependence on public assistance.

Many of the new jobs have already disappeared in the current
economic downturn. In hard times, service industries tend to decline
more rapidly than the economy as a whole. In addition, unemployment
has been aggravated by the following: (a) As noted, American industry
is being more effectively challenged by Asian and European competitors
than at any time in the postwar period. (b) Multinational corporations
have transferred many of their manufacturing operations from the United
States to parts of the world where labor costs are a fraction of what
they are in the United States. (one of the most threatening forms of
job transfer may be the use of satellite technology to facilitate the
transfer of corporate data and word processing operations to foreign
locations from which data can be communicated instantaneously and where
intelligent, inexpensive foreign labor can displace relatively well-
paid American office workers.) (c) The uncontrolled immigration of
millions of "illegal" immigrants, especially from Mexico and the Carib-
bean, who, because of a hopeless job situation at home, have attempted
to enter the United States in search of work.

In the midst of monumental technological and social transformations
which magnify the problem of population redundancy, the Reagan administration has initiated policies that have the effect of destroying the work
opportunities of millions of men and women while seriously reducing the
support given to the unemployed. Nor can it be said that these policies
are the result of high-level blundering or miscalculation. On the contrary, they are a form of economic triage initiated by political leaders
who believe in the Social Darwinist "survival of the fittest." As in
other forms of triage, resources are withheld from those who are incapable of helping themselves. There is reason to believe that America
is in the midst of a counter-revolution led by highly sophisticated opponents of the fifty-year-old welfare state who are honestly convinced
the current rise in unemployment and the reduction of welfare benefits
are in the nation's long-range interest.(31) The tradeoff between

unemployment and inflation has long been understood by macroeconomic planners. In the past, whenever inflation threatened to destabilize the economy, macroeconomic planners had a relatively simple way to lower prices, namely, to throw the economy into recession and thereby increase unemployment. Whatever the campaign rhetoric of politicians of both parties, the principal anti-inflation target of macroeconomic planners has been the labor force.

Toward the end of the nineteen-sixties, the strategy of trading off unemployment and inflation ceased to work as expected. Neither wages nor prices declined during recessions. It is now thought the new development was a consequence of the social-welfare programs enacted during the nineteen-sixties and seventies which shielded the poor from the worst effects of unemployment.(32) When the value of all health, subsistence, job training, and income maintenance programs were added up, few Americans found themselves forced to work simply to avoid hunger. The relative independence of the poor and the unemployed also strengthened the bargaining position of those within the work force.

As the nineteen-seventies came to an end, macroeconomic planners recognized that recessions could only play their historic role in reducing inflation if the bargaining position of the poor was weakened. This could only be achieved by reducing the support given to the poor and the unemployed by federal, state, and local government. Even the extraordinarily high deficit in the Reagan administration's budget helped to achieve this end. At first glance, it seemed strange that an administration claiming to be both conservative and fiscally responsible had proposed budgets with annual deficits exceeding $100,000,000,000. If, however, one perceives there is little that is genuinely conservative about this counter-revolutionary administration save, on occasion, its rhetoric, one will begin to comprehend why it has insisted on drastically reducing the national tax base while increasing both military spending and the budget itself. As Francis Fox Piven and Richard Cloward have suggested, the purpose of the deficit is so to mortgage the American future and limit the resources available to the federal government as to cripple its social-welfare programs, thereby stripping the poor of the economic protection they previously enjoyed.(33)

As structural unemployment has worsened in the United States, a massive underclass has arisen. I shall never forget a conversation I had recently with an intelligent seventeen-year-old young woman of Irish background at Boston's Commonwealth School. She told me why she had decided to attend a private shcool:

> "I considered myself a liberal. I had planned to go to a public high school, but what do you do when, at fifteen, most of your classmates are already third-generation welfare mothers? They have no interest in learning and it is impossible to learn anything in a class with them."

Private-school tuition is a tax hundreds of thousands of middle-class parents are currently paying because America has no viable way of coping with its underclass. Incidentally, the Commonwealth School does not discriminate against blacks or other minorities. Class rather than race was the crucial factor in the young woman's choice of school.

Apparently, the fifteen-year-old welfare mothers feel that state-supported single parenthood is the best option available to them. Given the grim alternatives available to the hopelessly poor, an adolescent's choice of a child of her own is by no means the least rational for the individual if not for society. Nor is the choice of crime or vice necessarily less rational for those without hope of gainful employment. This is in no sense a defense of crime or a plea to lessen vigilance in law enforcement. Crime and vice are obviously antisocial and must be dealt with as such. Nevertheless, they are often expressions of a socioeconomic predicament which is itself profoundly antisocial.

In spite of the spreading social pathology in America's cities, macroeconomic planners apparently do not regard the current level of unemployment as unacceptable. However, if unemployment continues to increase, crisis-ridden government leaders may eventually feel compelled to reconsider the ways in which the problem is to be managed. Should this happen, the probable scenarios are not very pleasant. When we consider them, we enter upon an effort to think about the unthinkable. Yet, lest we dismiss as implausible the grim scenarios we are about to consider, let us remember that the moral barriers which once prevented governments from eliminating large numbers of their own citizens have often been breached in the twentieth century. Although there is no need to indulge in unwarranted sensationalism or apocalypticism, much that is apocalyptic has already taken place in our century. Unfortunately, even more sorrowful misfortunes may await us if we permit ourselves the foolish luxury of pretending our problems are self-correcting.

It is obvious that the underclass has a certain utility as a reserve labor force. Nevertheless, in a period of acute economic hardship a future administration might conclude that mass unemployment and destitution no longer serve the national interest. If such a time ever comes, the problem of surplus people will admit of only two possible solutions: redistribution of resources and work opportunities or elimination of surplus people. In the past, most governments have chosen one form or another of the latter alternative, as the extraordinary emigration of Europeans to the New World demonstrates. Without the emigration opportunities available to nineteenth-century European governments, an American population-elimination program will, of necessity, be draconian, especially in view of the class, racial, religious, ethnic and ideological divisions pervading American life. Moreover, the depersonalized, value-neutral attitude toward job performance which characterizes bureaucratic administration will guarantee any government embarking on a draconian program that a body of competent functionaries stand ready to implement its policies. The

functional ethos will be reinforced by the heightened gravity of unemployment in a time when the unemployed are targeted for elimination.
Some functionaries may resist because of the dissonance between official policy and their personal values, but not enough to make a
practical difference. Whatever project government initiates, it will
not lack for willing personnel.

Since most Americans understandably find both redistribution and
population elimination unacceptable, we are likely to drift along in
the hope that the problem can somehow be managed without disturbing
the way of life of the working majority. In realty, the drift has
already proved costly in terms of the escalating incidence of vicious,
often gratuitous, criminality in America's cities, the cost of the
protective measures law-abiding citizens are compelled to take to
defend themselves, the spreading use of hard drugs, the rise of an
underground drug-based economy, and the massive deterioration of
large urban neighborhoods. The list is by no means inclusive.
Nevertheless, the phenomena of population redundancy and mass poverty
have already had a dramatic impact on the way of life of the average
American.

The possibility of finding a humane solution to the problems of
unemployment and poverty has been seriously weakened by the return to
respectability of Social Darwinism as a social philosophy among those
responsible for formulating the economic and social policies of the
current administration. Like Calvinism and the Neo-Malthusianism to
which it is related, Social Darwinism offers a rationale for the
felicity of an elect minority and the misfortune of the vast majority.
Social Darwinism can be seen as a form of secular Calvinism. What
Calvinists proclaim in the name of God, Social Darwinists assert in
the name of a strangely providential Nature.

In a time of acute socio-economic crisis, Social Darwinism, with
its application of the idea of the survival of the fittest to the
economic and social sphere, can provide decision-makers with a legit-
imating ideology for political decisions that spell disaster to
millions of their fellow citizens. Moreover, Social Darwinism is not
merely one ideology among many. It is a conceptualization of the pre-
theoretical foundations of the way most middle and upper class Americans
tend to view social reality. The plausibility of Social Darwinism is
greatly enhanced by its roots in both the predominant religious and
scientific traditions of American civilization. The dichotomous divi-
sion of society into the organization's insiders and the amorphous
mass of outsiders subject to its administration. Thus, unless we find
a humane way to solve the long-range problem of unemployment and population redundancy, we cannot rule out the possibility that in a crisis
we shall turn to inhumane methods under the spurious rationale that
the unemployed and the indigent are society's misfits and do not deserve to survive. Above all, we must not forget that even the worst
scenarios we can foresee as future possibilities have already taken
place in our century.

Is there then no escape from a situation in which millions of Americans become redundant and may eventually be eliminated altogether? It is my conviction that we are by no means helpless in meeting the challenge confronting us. While it is not my intention to offer a detailed prescription for the kinds of economic, political and social transformations required to meet the challenge, an indispensable requirement for averting social tragedy must be the restructuring of the American economy to provide a decent job for every American willing to work. Until private industry meets this need, we will have no alternative but to insist that provision of full employment become a permanent function of the federal government.

I find myself largely in agreement with economist Lester Thurow concerning the outlines of such a federal job program.(34) Thurow has suggested: (a) The program must offer all able-bodied Americans the kind of work opportunities and the range of earnings currently available to fully employed white males. (b) It must be designed to provide such work regardless of age, race, sex, and education. (c) The program must be seen as a permanent part of American life rather than a temporary expedient to help people weather a recession. This does not mean that all jobs in the program would be permanent. Some people would enter the program for short periods and some only on a part-time basis. Indeed, microcomputer automation may compel us to revise downward our understanding of what constitutes full-time work.

Our fundamental choice is between work and idleness. To date, we have chosen idleness whenever the private sector has been unable to make a profit. But this is an insane choice. Mass idleness and diminished productivity are infinitely more dangerous to the social fabric than enhanced productivity and full employment, whether brought about by the private or the public sector.

Obviously a government commitment to full employment will involve a massive restructuring of the economy. It will certainly involve changes in tax policy that would redirect the way money is invested. Such a program will inevitably be attacked as socialistic and even godless, as if an honest attempt to reduce the number of wasted American lives could ever be unholy. It is, however, not a proposal to dismantle private enterprise but to supplement it in those areas where the private sector has failed to function effectively. It is a serious effort to save and even to encourage the growth of those aspects of capitalism and private enterprise that are viable. We have already considered the possible ways American society might respond should the problem of unemployment continue to worsen. The scenarios are morally corrosive, destructive, and humanly wasteful. If sin has any social meaning, there can be few social phenomena more sinful than a society willing to tolerate the waste of millions of its citizens. Furthermore, even if it were possible forcibly to eliminate all of the "surplus" people, the problem would soon reappear with the progress of automation or with a change in the business cycle. In reality neither violence nor segregation of the unemployed can solve the problem.

A change in the way human beings sustain themselves, such as
would be entailed in a government-guaranteed full-employment program,
would affect almost every aspect of public and private life. As work
patterns are altered, so, too, would be patterns of leisure. As job
descriptions change, so, too, would job training. As work hierarchies
are altered, so, too, would social hierarchies. Art, literature and
music would soon reflect the transformations; so, too, would religion.
(In truth, it is my conviction that only a new religious consensus can
foster the civic altruism necessary to avert the monumental social
tragedy that may await us if we continue to ignore the root causes of
mass unemployment. I have little doubt that, if it is to remain a
viable society, America will achieve a religious consensus. I am not
currently able to suggest the outlines of such a consensus, although
Asian religions serve to remind us that a religious consensus need not
be a theistic consensus.)

It is my conviction that the proposed economic and social transformations constitute a conservative rather than a radical program.
There is nothing radical in attempting to halt mass despair before it
destroys civilization as we know it. There is nothing unholy about
seeking to maximize productivity with the help of government when the
private sector fails. Large corporations do it all the time. When
the middle class came to understand that higher education would remain
a monopoly of the rich and the religious without state support, they
turned to government to create the public university system. Is there
any reason why the state's resources can be used to educate the middle
class but not to rescue the unemployed from permanent worklessness?

There is nothing radical about insisting that no human being ought
to be considered surplus. On the contrary, the real radicals are those
who do not know the difference between a genuine human community and a
jungle. Survival of the fittest may indeed by the law of the jungle,
but a human community is not a jungle. Human beings have banded together to create an artificial space in which they can protect themselves from the ravages of the jungle and in which decency and civility
can govern the relations between them. When advocates of free-enterprise
capitalism and Social Darwinism naturalize the human condition and claim
that, as with all animals, the fundamental law of human existence is the
survival of the fittest, they are in reality insisting that even in
civil society the condition of mankind is one of the war of all against
all. They are the real radicals.

There is nothing conservative about a social philosophy that sub-
ordinates human relations to the impersonal and unpredictable tyranny
of the marketplace. What could be more radical or destructive of human
values than a society so organized that millions of men and women are
permanently denied any opportunity to lead productive lives? If we are
seriously interested in preserving private property in a complex, vulnerable high-technology civilization, we had better be prepared to abolish
welfare not by cutting the welfare budget but by providing job opportunities for all who are willing to work. A full-employment program is

neither radical nor utopian. On the contrary, it is the only viable response to the microelectronic revolution and to an explosive and morally corrosive social crisis.

Sooner or later, America will have a full-employment program. The only question is whether we are wise enough to initiate it before or after a monumental social tragedy. It is a sad fact of human nature that we are more likely to take corrective action after a tragic event than before. Yet, as we have noted throughout this essay, the tragic events we fear have already happened elsewhere. It remains to be seen whether they must happen to us before we take effective action.

(The material in this paper is taken from Richard L. Rubenstein, THE AGE OF TRIAGE: FEAR AND HOPE IN AN OVERCROWDED WORLD published by Beacon Press, Boston. No portion of this paper may be quoted or otherwise used without the permission of the author.)

THE STRANGERS AT OUR GATES:
REFUGEES FROM TERRORISM

ROGER WINTER

There have always been refugees. The better known refugees of
times past include the children of Israel and the Pilgrims. The
accoutrements of modern times have vastly complicated refugee matters
since their day. Now there are definitions and laws that apply. There
are techniques of modern civilization that implement persecution in
new-fangled ways. The decline of colonialism and the growth of nation-
states with defined borders left lines on maps that had no necessary
logical relationship to real-life human values. Useable vacant land
is disappearing. The world has divided into major ideological camps.
All of these--and the communications media--have complicated matters
in both helpful and hurtful ways.

Let us begin examining the modern refugee phenomenon with 1938.
Since World War I the international nature of refugee emergencies had
been increasingly recognized by the world community. But the legal,
organizational and political tools which should have accompanied this
new awareness were exceedingly weak.

And a boatload of Jews left Germany.

They were perceived by many to be the fortunate ones, bound for
sunny Cuba. Refugees normally are ordinary people in extraordinary
circumstances. If you know the story of the boat St. Louis, you know
the sequence of relief, drama, and ultimate horror that became the
fate of these otherwise ordinary people. Cuba didn't want them. The
St. Louis travelled 90 miles north sailing up and down within sight
of the lights of Miami, appealing for help. Our country's response
was to send out vessels primarily to be sure no one escaped the St.
Louis to enter the U.S. The ship finally returned to Europe where
many if not most of the Jews on board ultimately perished in the
Holocaust.

It took years after World II to resolve the fates of the thousands
displaced by the war. In 1951 the United Nations created the Office
of the UN High Commissioner for Refugees (UNHCR) to take international
leadership in seeking "durable solutions" regarding refugee situations.
Many of the nations of the world adopted the Convention on the Status
of Refugees, which had a limited definition of "Refugee" but which was
expanded by a Protocol in 1967 to refugees worldwide. The two documents, the UN Convention and Protocol, constitute the major modern
legal framework within which the international community responds to
refugees. Since most of you do not function day-to-day in refugee
matters, let's review the basics of that legal framework.

What is a "refugee" as defined by the Convention? All the world's poor longing for a better life are not refugees. All migrants or immigrants are not refugees. Refugees are not victims of natural disasters. Their disaster is man made. Refugees are people who are outside their country who have "...a well-founded fear of persecution on account of race, religion, nationality, membership in a particular social group, or political opinion..."

And what does an individual's inclusion in that definition do for that person? Not much in some cases. There are many reasons for this. One is that many countries have not acceded to the Convention and Protocol. Another is that determination of who meets the terms of the definition is entrusted to the nation in which the refugee is located. An example of the resulting confusion is the situation of many who have recently fled El Salvador. UNHCR generally considers them to be refugees. Some of the nations in which Salvadorans find themselves consider them illegal aliens.

What refugee status is supposed to confer is "non-refoulement." This is the principle of refugee protection that no refugee should be expelled from a nation in which he has found asylum back to the country he fled because of a "well-founded fear...". Refugee status also normally confers other legal and social rights such as permission to engage in employment.

The U. S. Committee for Refugees' World Refugee Survey for 1982 reflects a total of over 10 million refugees in the world, about three-quarters of whom are in need of relief and protection. The largest groupings are Afghans, Palestinians, Ethiopians, Salvadorans and Indochinese.

Those of us who work in this field see a hierarchy of so-called "durable solutions" in refugee emergencies, beyond the need for immediate relief and protection. I will not dwell on them here in detail, but topically the hierarchy is:

1. Voluntary repatriation to the home country under circumstances which provide adequate protection.

2. Resettlement in a neighboring country which offers asylum.

3. Resettlement in a third country, frequently distant from the home country.

As the word "hierarchy" implies, these solutions are ranked from most to least desirable from the international community's perspective.

Let us take a closer look for a moment at the classic third country resettlement episode of modern times. Zionist leader Chaim Weizmann noted on the eve of the Holocaust that, for the Jews of Europe, "the world is divided between countries in which they cannot live and countries which they may not enter." This was precisely the case with many Indochinese refugees in 1979. They were unable to return safely to their home countries, i.e. voluntary repatriation with adequate protection was not possible. The countries to which they were fleeing simply didn't want them. Boats were interdicted and turned back. Unseaworthy vessels were pushed back into the open sea. Malaysia indicated at one point that it would shoot refugees on sight. The Thais forceably repatriated over 40,000 Cambodians in one of the largest refugee tragedies of modern times. In sum, long-term resettlement in a neighboring country for these refugees was not a viable option.

But contrary to what happened to the Jews of the St. Louis, international pressure quickly came to bear on the front-line countries. Commitments were made by many countries to accept refugees for permanent resettlement if the front-line countries would offer them at least temporary asylum. Massive resettlement was initiated by the U. S., France, Canada, Australia, and others. There was no other viable alternative to prevent unlimited tragedy. It is in such a situation that third country resettlement is most in order. Most Americans took pride in these efforts.

But attitudes are changing within the American public. There are many reasons for this. These include the cumulative effects of the generally high levels of immigration we have experienced over the last several years, particularly high levels of illegal immigration, the downturn in the economy, and the Cuban boatlift of 1980.

The debate on the U. S. role in international refugee matters suffers from too much rhetoric on both sides. It is clouded by a lack of precision in terminology and concept which is unacceptable when dealing with people's lives and futures. Some have come to believe a refugee is "anyone who speaks a foreign language who is on welfare in my hometown." But refugees are unique, a distinct category of person who comes here from afar, characterized by vulnerability.

In my view, the principles of international protection for refugees are undergoing a period of degradation. And we, our people, have the ability to reverse that evil trend.

In the last 20 months we have seen the following happen:

1. Thailand has implemented a policy of "humane deterrence," splitting families and housing them in "austere camps" without opportunity for resettlement..

2. In June, Hong Kong implemented its own humane deterrence policy.

3. Salvadoran refugees have been pushed back into El Salvador with loss of life.

4. Djibouti has forced Ethiopian refugees back across the border.

5. Thailand has sealed its northwestern border to Lao hill-tribes
    people, forceably repatriated small groups of Lao to unknown
    fates, and is now implying it may forceably repatriate signfi-
    cant numbers of Cambodians.

All of this has occurred at a time when the U. S. and other nations
who have long championed human rights have reduced resettlement and implemented other restrictive policies. In the U. S., these have included
long-term detention of Haitians, interdiction of Haitians, and deportation of Salvadorans with what many believe are abridgments of due process and only perfunctory opportunity to claim asylum.

I certainly do not believe the U. S. can or should be expected to
admit for permanent resettlement here all who may wish to come. But
we must constantly be cognizant of how our nations contribute to the
strengthening or degradation of international standards of refugee
protection.

We have, I believe, several obligations in this context, including
the following:

1. Within whatever limits we as a nation choose to plan on
    immigration, priority must always be given to the truly
    vulnerable. Our admissions policy must be geared to
    supporting refugee protection worldwide. We cannot per-
    mit short-term political expediency to compromise long-
    term moral and humanitarian gain.

2. For those who directly seek asylum here, we owe them the
    opportunity to present their claim fully and to have that
    claim adjudicated fairly and equitably, with full respect
    for the implications of an erroneous decision to deny ad-
    mission.

3. As individuals and as a people, we must consciously promote
    the principles of human rights and protection for refugees
    and others. Unlike the elimination of war, establishment
    of adequate standards of international protection of refu-
    gees is achievable in the foreseeable future if the will
    to achieve it is exercised.

4. We must exorcize the dark phantoms of bias and prejudice,
    the fear of the different, the lack of concern about the
    stranger, which continue to blotch our collective psyche.
    The alien must not become the scapegoat for the ills that
    beset our society.

Although the goals I am setting for you to consider are an agenda
for the world community, our history make our own obligations in this

area unique. I would like to close with some words most of you will remember. They are the final lines of Ronald Reagan's acceptance speech at the convention that nominated him for President:

"I have thought of something that is not a part of my speech and worried over whether I should say it. Can we doubt that only a divine Providence placed this land, this island, the freedom here as a refuge for all those people in the world who yearn to be free. Jews and Christians enduring persecution behind the iron curtain, the boat people of Southeast Asia, Cuba and Haiti, the victims of drought and famine in Africa, the freedom fighters in Afghanistan...Can we begin our crusade joined together in a moment of silent prayer for these people."

Such prayer, and the concrete actions which must accompany it, are the necessary steps that must be taken to avoid the kind of tragedy that this conference focuses on in hindsight.

THE RESPONSE OF INSTITUTIONALIZED

RELIGION TO THE HOLOCAUST

DR. ROBERT W. ROSS

The information, analysis and conclusions contained in So It Was
True: The American Protestant Press and the Nazi Persecution of the Jews
were obtained from a sample of fifty-two Protestant religious periodicals
published during the Nazi era, 1933-1945. On several pertinent issues,
some periodicals were examined up to 1950 (See Appendix A, 353-355).
This sample represents @ 1,000 such periodicals published during the
1930s and 1940s with an estimated readership of above 30,000,000 (see
Marty, Deedy, Silverman and Lekachman, The Religious Press in America,
New York, Holt, Rinehart and Winston, 1963 for more detailed information).

Several criteria were established to control the sample. The periodicals were to represent all parts of the Protestant community, large
and small, denominational, interdenominational and undenominational,
nationally circulated and available to the average reader who might receive the publication. Most of the denominational periodicals were circulated to members of the local congregations affiliated with the organization, i.e. The Baptist Herald for members of the German Baptists of
North America, The Gospel Messenger to members of the Church of the
Brethren, The Presbyterian to members of the Presbyterian Church in the
USA, etc. The undenominational periodicals were sold by direct subscrip-
tion or in some instances through local congregations in addition to the
denominational periodical, such as The Sunday School Times, The Christian
Century, The Christian Herald or The Moody Bible Institute Monthly.

Such sampling is called "purposive sampling: and is within the dis-
ciplined inquiry of the content analysis of print media. A "purposive
sample" is characterized by the following: 1) 100% of the items examined
are used, even if, as in the case of The Banner Herald (Primitive Baptist)
no information is found. That fact is pertinent information; 2) the
sample speaks for itself, i.e. what is found is what is reported; and 3)
any evaluation, analysis, conclusions, synthesis or comments about the
sample and what is found in it are made as "end" remarks in each chapter
and, as in So It Was True as separate chapters where some attempt at
"meaning" is made (see Part II, Chapters 7 and 8, 263-301).

The emphasis on "read," or at least "received" in the homes of con-
stituent members or subscribers is important. Wide dissemination of the
information, in this instance what American Protestant Christians knew
about what was happening to Jews in Germany must be shown over a wide
readership, over a significant span of time (12+ years) and over a wide
range of Protestant groups. The sample proved rich in its yield in all
three categories. The readership, potentially, was extremely wide based
on numbers of periodicals circulated, the time span covered the years of

Hitler's dictatorship, 1933-1945 and the range of Protestant groups was more than adequate to be representative.

From this data base then, the pertinent information was obtained, concerning the Nazi persecution of the Jews (1933-1939) and about the Holocaust years (1939-1945). The information obtained was directed toward a central question; who knew what, when and in what detail? This same question was also asked by two other scholars whose books were published in 1980, as was So It Was True. Walter Laqueur looked at information in foreign office archives in the European countries of Allied nations and neutral countries and into information obtained through the Polish underground, by the International Red Cross in Geneva and to some extent what was known in Palestine. He focussed on the years 1940-1942. His findings were published in 1980 as The Terrible Secret.

John Morley examined what was known by the Vatican through examining correspondence between the Vatican Secretary of State, Cardinal Maglione, and the Vatican's official representatives in the major cities of countries occupied by the Nazis, concentrating on the years 1939-1943. His book, Vatican Diplomacy and the Jews During the Holocaust Years was also published in 1980. All three books, using entirely different data bases, came to the same general conclusion. All information about what was happening to Jews in Germany, including ghettoization, disease, starvation, firing squad mass killing, the gas chambers and the forced labor system of the concentration camps was fully known by the Western world, including the general public. In addition, So It Was True, since it covered the entire Hitler era in contrast to the shorter time span of Laqueur and Morley, documents the knowledge that American Protestants had from their own publications about the Nazi persecution of the Jews from 1933 to 1939.

Protestant Christians knew very early about the plight of the Jews in Germany. The first notice of persecution of Jews was recorded for the date February 13, 1933 (see p.6). The April 1, 1933, pogrom and boycott of Jewish businesses was reported in some detail to American Protestant Christians (see p.9-10). The "Aryan clause" later to be incorporated into the Nuremberg Laws, was reported with a discussion of implications for Jews in Germany, and with recorded protest of the action, (see p.13-18). There were also some rather remarkable statements made or articles written that can only be described as pro-German, in the Protestant press of 1933, (example: p.10-11).

Protestant Christians not only knew early what the plight of the Jews was in Germany, but they also were informed in detail. Probably no published document in period 1933-1939 is as detailed and comprehensive as the James G. McDonald Letter of Resignation and "Annex" published as a supplement to the January 15, 1936, issue of The Christian Century. Totalling twenty-seven pages, in all, the Letter (three pages) and the "Annex" (twenty-four pages) analyze the effect of the Nuremberg Laws of September 15, 1935, on Germany's Jews. McDonald's analysis and perceptions are nothing less than astonishing considering the relatively early date of the publication. Read after-the-fact, that is after 1945, McDonald was prescient if not almost prophetic. If what he wrote was astonishing in its accuracy and clarity, the fact that what he wrote was virtually totally ignored by the League of Nations and by the nations of the world is equally astonishing, (see p.81, 84-89, 118-119).

By the same token, Kristallnacht, the Night of the Broken Glass, November 9-13, 1938, was fully reported in the Protestant religious press. All details and aspects of the event were reported in full. Grynszpan and Vom Rath were named, the resulting anti-Jewish mob actions reported, the extent of the damage throughout Germany and in Austria described and protests and actions taken, mainly ignored, by the nations of the West, (see p.109-121).

It may then be further stated, that Protestant Christians in America knew everything that was made public from any source whatsoever, in the years 1939-1945. The Watchman-Examiner for December 28, 1939, reported the existence of a place which they called a "Jewish preserve" near Lublin in Poland to which large numbers of Jews were already being transported from Vienna and Bohemia-Moravia, (see p.143).

Ghettoization of Jews in Poland was reported, as was the existence of concentration camps and the forced labor system throughout Germany, in Poland, France and Holland. Ghettoization of Jews in the Baltic countries was also reported. Mass deportation of Jews was reported beginning in 1941, and by 1942, these transports of mass numbers of Jews to unknown destinations "in the East" as "resettlement" were already being linked to some sort of mass extermination process, the "poison chambers" of the letter of Rabbi Hertz, (see p.162). The details of what was known by Protestant Christians in America from their own press by the end of the year 1942, is summarized (see p.163-164), but also a summary of what was not known is also included in these pages. They did not know of the directives written to instigate the "Final Solution of the Jewish Problem," nor the names of the persons involved at the highest levels of the Nazi leadership, nor the names of the "killing centers." This information would become known later.

By 1944, the "more atrocity stories" problem, the legacy of World War I, had clearly moved to the central place as a problem for editors of the Protestant press. Many remembered, and referred to the atrocity stories of World War I as the basis for their caution or outright skepticism in the face of more and more evidence from Europe that mass extermination was taking place. Who is credible? Who can be believed? Where are the trained professionals, journalists and others who can finally verify what we are hearing? Henry Smith Leiper, in Advance (Congregational), addressed this dilemma directly. "A message...from a very responsible and well-informed friend in Europe indicates that the tales that come out of unhappy Poland are not mere rumors or atrocity stories," (see p.172).

Controversy also arose concerning verifiable information, use of sources for such information, the role of the U.S. government, especially the State Department, and what could be proven as fact. The well-known independent periodical The Christian Century was involved in such a public disagreement with Rabbi Stephen S. Wise. The Century disputed Wise, who had released information about the extent of the extermination of Jews in Europe, and the position of the Century was that none of this information could be verified, and in fact, the U. S. State Department denied the accuracy of Wise's information, upon inquiry from the Century. At this juncture the central position of the Allies concerning Jews in Europe began to be expressed. "The only way to help the Jews is to win the war."

By 1944, no surprises remained. Majdanek, one of the extermination centers near Lublin, was liberated by the Russians. This camp and its functions were widely reported to the world because the Russians invited a select group of professional journalists, thirty in all, to visit Majdanek and to tell the story, (see p.199-202); Majdanek only completed, or confirmed what had already been reported, including the name Auschwitz as the site of a death camp (see p.199). As stated, "No part of the Nazi-instigated plan was left out. Deportation, massacres, ghettos, gas chambers, crematori starvation, disease, 'firing squads,' gas vans, medical experiments, transport trains, brutality, mass graves and trenches, and death camps were reported" (see p.202).

Only the final, awful confirmation remained, that of finding of the concentration camp and forced labor system, filled with emaciated Jews and others and with the bodies of the unburied and unburned lying about in profusion to elicit the responses typical in the editorials and articles in the Protestant press in April and May of 1945. Charles Clayton Morrison of The Christian Century called it "Gazing Into the Pit," (see p.228-229); The New York Herald-Tribune and The Churchman used "The Shape of Buchenwald" as their title, (see p.231); the editor of The Signs of the Times used "So It Was True," concluding, "Yes, it is all too true," (see p.233). The cautious and unconvinced remained, and the plainly skeptical wrote of their skepticism even in the face of the overwhelming evidence, (see p.236-238). And the witnesses stepped forward quickly. They were American servicemen in units of the U. S. Army that found the camps and the inmates, and who wrote letters to their denominational papers, distinguished American churchmen who visited Europe very soon after the Nazis were driven out, both before the war ended and immediately after the war ended, and prominent civic and government leaders. General Eisenhower invited them to come as verifica tion of what was discovered. And the press was everywhere. The pictures of emaciation and of death filled the papers, magazines and newsreels. Photo exhibits were prepared and mounted in London and in the U. S. The correspondent for The Lutheran Standard from Washington, D.C. refers to having visited such an exhibit, (see p.235).

The Epilogue (see p.258-259) raises the critical questions; the first of the two concluding chapters carefully reviews and summarizes the amount of information published in the American Protestant press from 1933 to 1945 and after. "Each one of these reported events stands as a witness that

American Protestant Christians were informed by their own press about the Nazi persecution (and extermination) of the Jews," (see p.284). The second concluding chapter, the last in the book, raises the more critical question of the inaction of American Protestant Christians in any effective way, and what has been called "the Silence" by Jews. Two conclusions are noted. The first is that "the Silence" does not mean lack of knowledge or sparsity of information. There was, in fact, not as much of a "silence" as had been thought to be the case, the assumption being that nothing was done because no one knew what was happening. The evidence reported in So It Was True completely undermines this conclusion.

What, then, does "the Silence" mean? Five different meanings are assigned to this term to verify its usefulness and its accuracy: the failure to persuade; the failure of concerted effort; the failure of modest actions; the failure of World War II as an intervention for Jews; and the failure to speak in "Moral Passion." The last meaning of "the Silence" is then contrasted to the response of the American Protestant press when the Atom Bomb was dropped in Japan. No such moral outrage, or mass outcry came upon discovering the destruction of 12,000,000 people, 6,000,000 of whom were Jews, after V-E day. It is a strange, but significant point, this sharply delineated response to those two cataclysmic events. A few spoke to the issue, but very few.

Finally, the words of Hilaire Belloc, quoted by Robert A. Ashworth on September 21, 1933, in The Reformed Church Messenger proved prophetic, (see p.300).

Two surprises, really significant discoveries were made while doing the research for So It Was True. The first was the amazing clarity, understanding and foresight of the problems facing Jews in Germany, and as later proved true, throughout Europe, of James G. McDonald. It may almost be stated categorically that if no other document had been published in the American Protestant press than his "Letter of Resignation" and accompanying "Annex" (The Christian Century, January 15, 1936 Supplement), this would be enough to base the conclusion on, that American Protestant Christians knew early, and they knew enough about the plight of the Jews, that they cannot say they did not know.

The second surprise was of a different sort altogether. It requires a brief explanation. Through evangelistic efforts by some Protestant groups, what in German is called Judenmission, occasionally a Jew will become a convert to Christianity. From a Jewish perspective such a person is no longer a Jew. Such is not the case with the convert, thus the hyphenate Hebrew-Christian or Jewish-Christian. Sometime, such a convert, or Hebrew-Christian will become engaged in evangelistic work among Jews, either in the U. S. or in Europe and often in alliance with or as a member of an organization specifically engaged in such a task, i.e. a "mission to the Jews."

Beginning early in 1934 (February) such organizations began to purchase advertising space in Protestant religious periodicals, particularly those of a conservative, or evangelical, or Fundamentalist bent. These paid advertisements appeared regularly from 1934 through 1945 and after, and their value is that they consistently told about what was happening to Jews in Germany, Poland and throughout Europe. The information was being sent to them from their own sources within Europe, often their own missionaries who were on the site and who sent the information back to the U. S. in personal letters.

The information contained in these ads is among the earliest and the most accurate information we now have available to use, reporting about the plight of the Jews in Europe. Their's was a personal interest, expressed unreservedly often in full-page ads. What is also significant is that the periodicals selling the ad space to these organizations either seldom, or never contained any other information about the plight of Europe's Jews. There were no editorials, articles or even comments, yet they would make the space available on a regular basis, and did so for almost twelve years.

But, surprises aside, the central assertion of So It Was True remains. Protestant Christians in America, if they read their own periodicals (and many did) knew early, and they potentially knew everything about what was happening to Jews in Germany and throughout most of Europe during the Hitler years, 1933-1945. Only in 1945 at the end of World War II did the immensity of the war against the Jews and the crime against humanity become fully apparent, but Protestant Christians in America cannot say that they did not know.

CREATING HUMANE PHYSICIANS

ALTON I. SUTNICK, M.D.

Walter Lippmann, the great journalist and political philosopher, wrote in 1913 (1), "Whether we wish it or not, we are involved in the world's problems and all the winds of heaven blow through our land." Of course, he was referring to the inescapable involvement of the United States in the gathering warclouds of Europe but that comment could refer to all of our interests as they interact with our socio-political environment. Certainly, many aspects of our society are inextricably involved in other parts of the world. Because of rapid communications and appreciation of what has gone on in the past, the sensitivity to the Holocaust is bound to continue.

How can the medical education community advance a goal of a more just, peaceful world? How does medical education get involved in that? We try to shape our institutions as very human types of institutions. We try to produce doctors who value human relationships. We try to produce doctors who are going to teach others and who will replicate intellectual descendants who have similar values. That is an important goal for us.

How does one proceed to attain such a goal? There are various points in the educational process at which it can be addressed. The first is the selection of the students from among the applicants. The second is the creation of the atmosphere in which they are going to learn--an atmosphere that will help them to value human relation-ships. Third is the approach to teaching, and fourth, demonstrating what the administration of the medical school and its faculty do to protect those values, the establishment of role models for the students.

There has been considerable interest in the lay press recently about the selection of medical school applicants to become the kind of doctors that we want to have. Certainly academic achievements are important. It is necessary to have the capacity and the basic skills for studying and absorbing material and for entering a lifelong learn-ing process that doesn't stop when you graduate medical school. But we also put considerable emphasis on the personal interview, the let-ters of recommendation, particularly those that address the kind of person that this potential medical student is (2). We ask our inter-viewers to look at this applicant and consider how they would like this person if they were lying in a hospital bed and this was their doctor. The applicants are asked about their interests in under-graduate college activities outside of academic concerns. They are asked about their service to organizations in which they have been involved, their relationships to their families and friends, the

origin of their interest in medicine. This is an attempt to determine their personal characteristics that would make them good all-
around physicians. We find our current students to be very responsible, understanding people, interested in society but not to the
exclusion of their main effort as students. Many medical schools
use their own students as part of the recruiting process for new
students. We try to perpetuate the kind of student body that we
already have.

Then we want to create an atmosphere for learning in which
human relationships are important. We want the student to feel
valued as a real person and not just a number in the class. We
strive for strengthening personal interactions between classmates,
between students in different classes, between faculty in different
departments and between faculty and students. At The Medical College of Pennsylvania, we try to maintain an informal, personal type
of atmosphere, an intimate relationship between people (2). It
takes a lot of effort; it just doesn't happen. It is something that
we have established as a priority. I believe it is an important
goal for medical schools to meet, to provide a suitable environment
for medical students to develop an appreciation of human concerns
and needs.

Our students subscribe to an honor code. We endorse the principle of mutual respect and responsibility for honesty and faithful
performance among students, between faculty and students as the
foundation of later professional autonomy and peer review. They
are obligated to "police" themselves for honest, high performance--
as they will need to do in the practice of medicine later.

One of the first objects with which the medical student has
experience is the human body. In his book, THE ANATOMY LESSON,
Marshall Goldberg vividly describes the gross anatomy laboratory,
and expresses an important thought through the words of the anatomy
professor on the students' first day (3). He says, "You are dealing
with the bodies of unfortunate souls, whose remains went unclaimed--
people who have passed tragically through life leaving nothing of
any material value behind, and few who might miss or mourn them. I
am certain that if one of us had been able to tell them beforehand
that in death their bodies would make a contribution of the highest
order to humanity, through you the medical student, they would have
been exceedingly gratified. Their bodies deserve your respect. We
demand it, and needless to say, we unfailingly receive it." This
is an important message that we feel students should receive on
their first day in medical school.

Throughout medical school the students are urged to treat
patients with dignity. They are taught to respect their patients'
needs, to try and understand them as people, not only as a classi-
fication of disease.

At The Medical College of Pennsylvania, we have a Medical Humanities program which incorporates bioethics and various aspects of humanities into the future physician's education (4). The program includes a required course in bioethics in the first year and a series of elective courses through the rest of the four years of medical school. About 25 to 30 percent of students take advantage of those electives--electives such as Death and Dying, the History of Medicine, the Philosophy of Science, Literature in Medicine, Art in Medicine, and Bioethics in Clinical Care (for Juniors and Seniors). Whether these courses meet in very informal settings in the homes of faculty members in the evenings, or in campus classrooms, they generate in people who are progressing through medical school reflective thinking that ties medicine directly to life. We think that is an important thing to do. In addition to the courses, there are Humanties Grand Rounds on a regular basis. For the past five years, Humanities Fellows in various fields (including history, philosophy and art) have been invited to spend a year at the College in an effort to expand the threshold of learning of medical students, and to help them to deepen their understanding of the relationship of their own scholarly discipline to the potential concerns of clinical medicine.

There are other aspects of medical school activities that relate to the interests of society. One is the protection of human subjects in biological research, which is carefully regulated in the medical school setting.

A standing committee is mandated, to include lay members, to review protocols of all proposed research projects involving human subjects and to recommend modifications consistent with maintaining the highest degree of safety. It may be necessary to interdict some protocols. The penalties for not submitting to this review are severe. Approval is required before the research is initiated. The subject must be fully informed of the procedures involved in the study before agreeing to participate.

At the time the students graduate, they take an oath to conduct their professional lives in an ethical way. One of the commonly used oaths is the Oath of Maimonides (5). At the conclusion of discussion of this subject, it is useful to read that oath carefully because in many ways, it exemplifies the way they should develop their lives and careers.

"Thy eternal providence has appointed me to watch over the life and health of Thy creatures. May the love for my art actuate me at all times; May neither avarice nor miserliness nor thirst for glory, or a great reputation engage my mind; for the enemies of truth and philanthropy could easily deceive me and make me forgetful of my lofty aim of doing good to Thy children. May I never see in the patient anything but a fellow creature in pain. Grant me strength, time and opportunity always to correct what I have acquired, always to extend its domain; for knowledge is immense and the spirit of man can extend indefinitely to enrich itself daily with new requirements. Today he can discover his errors of yesterday and tomorrow he can obtain a new light on what he thinks himself sure of today. O God, Thou has appointed me to watch over the life and death of Thy creatures, here I am ready for my vocation and now I turn unto my calling."

REFERENCES

1. Lippmann, W. A Preface to Politics. University of Michigan Press.
    Ann Arbor, Chapter 4, 1913.

2. Sutnick, A.I. A look to the future in medical school admissions.
    Alumnae/i News 31:2-5, 1981.

3. Goldberg, M. The Anatomy Lesson. Berkeley Publishing Corp.,
    New York, p. 32, 1974.

4. Sorenson, J.H., Bergman, G.E. and Sutnick, A.I. Teaching humanities
    in medical school: the experience of The Medical College of Penn-
    sylvania. Forum on Medicine 31:114-118, 1980.

5. Maimonides, Moses. The Oath of Maimonides.

"THE DEBASED COIN OF COMMUNICATIONS"

A. H. RASKIN

I am delighted to be the kickoff speaker in this workshop session aimed at marshalling the brainpower of those of us in communications, education, technology, business, labor, the law, medicine and the full panoply of professions to guard against the omnipresent threat of thermonuclear annihilation and, no less urgent, to build an affirmative framework of understanding and cooperation for the benefit of all humanity.

In many respects, there never has been a more propitious time for undertaking this monumental mission, a time when the potentialities for success were so great. Many of you will undoubtedly consider that a dubious, not to say fatuous, remark to come from one who, through all his professional career, was almost invariably to be found prominent among the prophets of gloom and doom--so much so, indeed, that I served with great pride on the editorial board of THE NEW YORK TIMES through all the turbulent years in which President Nixon and Vice President Agnew were letting no day go by without inveighing against us and our counterparts on THE WASHINGTON POST as "nattering nabobs of negativism."

The basis for my sanguinity is that we are coming into what has rightly been touted as "the age of the mind"--a period in which revo-lutionary developments in telecommunications are giving us the tools with which to make a reality of the Information Society, to banish illiteracy and to broaden the horizons of knowledge everywhere. What remains in question--and here I profess no optimism whatsoever--is whether we have the will and wisdom to apply these gifts of science in ways that will serve the needs and aspirations of people everywhere or whether they will be chained to considerations of profit in a manner that confines to those who can pay the price the enjoyment of these vast powers of enlightenment and emancipation. Through the marriage of satellites, lasers, fiber optics and computers, the facilities available to us for the exchange of information and ideas are limitless. Our poverty is in the imagination--or, more accurately, the lack of imagination--with which we propose to apply that capacity. As of now, most of our ingenuity is focussed on its utilization for Atari games, an infinite variety of narrow-cast business services and a multiplica-tion in entertainment-for-pay programs with a heavy tilt toward the bluest of pornography.

In the perspective of this conference, no challenge seems to me more urgent than a search for methods to reverse the trend almost everywhere in public life toward debasing the coin of communication. We are still, so far as the calendar goes, two years away from George Orwell's 1984, but Doublespeak is already well-entrenched as the rule in political discourse nationally and internationally. Words seem to have lost all meaning except as vehicles for sophistry and deceit.

We have certainly seen that with depressing regularity in this
election season. Compassion for the plight of the unemployed has
been turned on and off like a faucet. One day our President exults
in an ephemeral surge in stock prices as a rebuke to the hawkers of
gloom in the opposite party. The next day he commandeers TV time to
remind us that he is a child of the Great Depression and that no
heart bleeds more than his for the suffering of the jobless. He
is not going to play "the blame game," he assures us, after weeks
of proclaiming that all the nation's economic woes are a heritage
he is trying to erase of the malpractices of the Democrats, with their
profligate adherence to the philosophy of hyperactive government.

The Democrats, for their part, have not been above reveling in
the unemployment figures and every other evidence of economic distress.
They have borrowed a leaf from the old Communist handbook that the
worse things get, the better for our side, because only when we hit
bottom will people rise in their wrath and heave out the whole rotten
crowd. Certainly, not one bill passed this year or last in the Demo-
cratic-controlled House would have made any significant difference
had it won concurrence in the Republican Senate and been signed by
President Reagan.

What cause for wonder, given this politics-as-usual attitude
in both major parties as we stagger under a mountain of wasted man-
power and unused productive resources unparalleled since the calami-
tous 1930s, that there is so much defeatism among the jobless in all
our great industrial centers. The frequency with which workers in-
terviewed while they wait disconsolately to register for unemployment
insurance say they are not going to vote this year because they have
no confidence in the promises or prospective performance of either
Republicans or Democrats signals a loss of faith in the democratic
process that we in communications and the professions cannot ignore.

It is reflective of the deeper mistrust that has been growing
in this country for more than a decade. This mistrust is a product
of Vietnam, of Watergate, of Abscam, of the daily parade of indict-
ments of public officials, judges, police officers and other betrayers
of governmental trust. In industry and labor and in most other sections of public affairs, the climate is no more exhilarating, the
moral standards equally dreary. "Everything is a ripoff. Why should
I try to do what's right when everybody else is stealing with both
hands?" has become the watchword for millions of Americans.

Nor is any relief from such cynicism to be found by turning our
eyes outward. Mendacity makes a mockery of many of our professed
positions as worldwide champions of human rights and of justice,
rather than force, as the determinant in disputes among nations. The
President issues and Congress meekly acquiesces in phony certifica-
tions that progress is being made toward abolishing right-wing terror
of El Salvador at a time when even the most moderate reformers there

are in constant danger of violent death. We applaud the gallant
struggle of Polish workers for the rudiments of freedom, but the
sanctions we seek to apply against the military governors of Poland
and their masters in the Kremlin are so quixotic and so clearly
dictated by considerations of domestic political advantage that it
is hard to blame our European allies for behaving with comparable
opportunism.

The tragedy is that in this interdependent world, on the threshold of the establishment of outposts in space and under the surface
of the oceans, neither we nor any other country, East or West, North
or South, is exhibiting any consistent concern, much less originality,
in developing a more dependable foundation for cooperation to assure
peace and economic stability. The United Nations, brought into being
with such brave hopes less than four decades ago, is a shambles. How
long the United States will even stay a member is at this moment very
much a question. The U.N.'s impotence and the manifest unfairness of
many U.N. positions have, in any event, discredited it to an extent
that makes it improbable that it will ever succeed in enshrining sanity
as the touchstone in international relations.

Yet exactly twenty years ago, we were all living under the mush-
room cloud of the crisis precipitated by President Kennedy's demand
that Nikita Khrushchev remove Soviet missiles from Cuba. The President himself rated the chances as 50-50 that the upshot would be
nuclear war. Recent developments in the Middle East have reminded
us for the thousandth time of how easy it is for even the most responsible of governments to find rationalizations in what their
leaders consider matters of national security and survival for actions that make distressingly clear the fragility of the defenses
any of us have against a new holocaust.

Our ability to grapple with these problems, domestic and international, is gravely undermined--if not destroyed--by the debasement
in the currency of communication about which I talked at the outset.
So long as our leaders and those of the rest of the world slither
around in a quicksand of hypocrisy where practice rarely bears much
resemblance to preachment and where yo-yo swings in stated position
are incessant, we will not have the foundation of trust essential
for any enduring society or any society worthy of enduring. Indeed,
without that irreplaceable bedrock of trust, there can be no social
impact and therefore nothing that might properly be called a society.

Much as I respect the collective talents of those of us gathered
in this workshop, candor compels me to acknowledge that converting
the movers and shakers of government and industry to universal observance of the Golden Rule is likely to exceed our immediate reach.
But I do think that we in communications can make at least a minute
beginning along that line, and I am sure you in the other professions
have much to offer beyond doleful head-shaking toward advancing our

goal of a more just and peaceful world.

The priority I assign to communications stems not solely from the fact that it is the profession in which I have spent my life but, even more, from the steadily mounting awareness that a half-century of involvement at every level from campus correspondent to editor has brought me of the degree to which the mass media have contributed to mistrust, misunderstanding and misinformation, all in the name of service to the general good. My sense that something is sorely skewed in the fulfillment of our indispensable role as eyes and ears for the community keep growing even though it was my good fortune through the great bulk of my career to be associated with a newspaper that strives earnestly to live up to its reputation as the exemplar of all that is best in journalistic responsiblity.

Part of the problem, I am afraid, lies in our definition of news as something out of the ordinary—a compendium of the aberrational in the events of the day. The easy explanation—but one I find less than totally persuasive—for this decision to ignore as routine almost everything that bespeaks stability in human affairs is that the complexity of modern life creates happenings of such range and volume that reporters and editors must exercise selectivity to keep the citizenry from being snowed under. To be sure, newspapers and TV news round-ups cannot function in the manner of vacuum cleaners dumping their accumulation of dribble on your breakfast table or into your living room in great undigested gobs. The Associated Press alone moves 3 million words of news copy in a single day, and gatekeepers at every news organization must choose what to use out of that heavy tide, supplemented as it is by the fruits of the independent digging of their own staffs and of countless special news and features syndicates.

What bothers me is that the focus on the bizarre and the unorthodox in what is selected has the inescapable effect of viewing society through a funhouse mirror that distorts the image the public receives of the world and community in which we live. Please don't interpret that as a plea on my part for "happy news," that abomination of newscasters who find something to joke about in the direst of developments. Rather, my complaint is with the lack of perspective that too often blocks the understanding journalism should give Americans as the basis for responsible approaches to their own lives and for intelligent decisions on matters of public policy.

A particularly illuminating discussion of this failure of the press to supply the citizens with information in a manner calculated to fit it into context and promote comprehension has just come from the man who startled us all a year ago with his article in THE ATLANTIC on "The Education of David Stockman." He is William Greider, then national editor of THE WASHINGTON POST, who has now written what amounts to "The Education of William Greider" in the October issue of THE WASHINGTON MONTHLY.

In it he tells of his shock at the way in which his ATLANTIC article was treated in the media. Here is an excerpt: "A long and complex narrative, constructed to preserve subtlety and ambiguity, was swiftly rendered into tart little capsules, the choicest nuggets of 'news' that might provoke and embarrass. I could hardly quarrel with the accuracy of the technique (having practiced it myself for many years), but it disappointed me." What disappointed him most-- and this goes to the heart of my complaint--is that almost no attention was given at any stage of the flurry over the Stockman article to the deeper questions raised by the Budget Director's account of governing.

Greider's gripe is one made every day of the week by politicians and figures in public life all over the country. In their desire to get the "big hit" story, journalists concentrate on the elements that will titillate the public, those that will simplify or startle, to the exclusion of what is of genuine consequence. In the process an incestuous relationship develops between newspeople and their sources, which fosters fakery and defeats understanding.

I do not want to overstep the boundaries of your patience by delving in depth into the evils of character assassination based on information from unidentified sources, outright hoaxes of the kind perpetrated by Janet Cooke in her fictitious account of "Jimmy's World" or the many other abuses that have sapped the media's credibility and contributed to the spread of Doublespeak by our governmental leaders.

Let me just say, in preparing to close, that I have long felt there was all too much warrant for the widespread popular feeling that journalism, especially in these days of one-newspaper cities and concentrated ownership of all the major instruments of communication, is too powerful and too often irresponsible in the exercise of that power. It has never seemed to me that the immunity which the freedom-of-the-press clause of the First Amendment wisely gives the media against governmental control or intrusion should be twisted into an excuse for insistence by the press that it ought to be the one institution in our society that should be totally exempt from any form of accountability.

That is why I have been happy in the five years since my departure from THE NEW YORK TIMES to be a staff officer of THE NATIONAL NEWS COUNCIL, the nearest thing we have in the United States to an agency of accountability monitoring the accuracy and fairness of the press, both print and electronic. It is a place to go for individuals or organizations who feel they have been shafted in a news story or broadcast--a place where they can get an impartial assessment of the validity of their complaint from a panel of 18 members, all with distinguished records of accomplishment in the media and in civic affairs. It is nongovernmental and noncoercive. It has no power to enforce sanctions, and desires none. It relies totally on the force of public opinion to give substance to its decisions.

Regrettably, the effectiveness of the Council and its usefulness
as an instrument of redress for aggrieved citizens are severely
limited by the fact that, even now in the tenth year of its existence,
conservatively 99 percent of the population is aware that there is
such an organization. The near-blackout that attends media attention
to our findings is itself a commentary on the subjective and often
self-protective standards that govern what is news, as determined
by the gatekeepers who are the final arbiters of what you read and
see. A willingness within the media to re-examine the soundness of
those standards would be an excellent starting point for the endeavor
to introduce more honesty into political discourse and to rebuild
faith in the integrity of the coin of communications.

SIGNS OF OPPRESSION: PRE-NAZI GERMANY - PRESENT DAY REALITY

THEODORE R. MANN, ESQUIRE

In these times in which varying views on the subject of the Middle
East are held with such great intensity and passion, I find more and
more that I had better tell my audience up front that I am speaking on
only one aspect of a very complex situation, and if I fail to express
their most cherished beliefs or sense of outrage, it is only because it
is not germane to the topic.

So, tonight, before I express to a Christian and Jewish audience
a view of that awful event in Lebanon, let me make clear that while I
share with many of you the feeling that Israel has been treated out-
rageously by a hypocritical world in the past several months, I will
not refer to that subject again because it is irrelevant to the primary
points I want to make this evening, to which I will now turn.

We could not hold a Holocaust Conference in October, 1982, without
taking note of a massacre in Lebanon in September, 1982, and without
trying to derive from it some lesson, some instruction, that will help
us mitigate the slaughter and the degradation which some members of the
human family continue to perpetrate on other members of the human family
even now--40 years after the destruction of the six million.

Last month, hundreds of Palestinian refugees in two refugee camps
in Lebanon--including women, children and old men--were massacred in
cold blood. The perpetrators were Lebanese who obscenely choose to
call themselves Christians. They were permitted entry into the camp
by the Israeli military. According to the Israeli military, the Lebanese
were permitted entry in order to find PLO terrorists who had managed to
remain behind when many thousands of their fellows left Lebanon a week
earlier. So much for the bare facts.

We derive some instruction from the events of the following week.
You will recall that the Israeli prime minister and its minister of
defense initially disclaimed all responsibility, and refused to authorize an independent investigation of all the facts surrounding the massacre. After the Israeli Press insisted on a full investigation, and
after the Israeli President--a largely ceremonial office--insisted on
a full investigation and after 400,000 angry citizens, many of them
survivors of the Holocaust, took to the streets and insisted on a full
investigation, Prime Minister Begin ordered a full investigation, which
is now in process. We learn from this, of course, the value of a free
and a vigorous press and that is no small thing. No American newspapers
were as hard on the Israelis as was the Israeli press. But I would remind you that notwithstanding the outcry of the Israeli press, and notwithstanding President Navon's demands, the Knesset supported the Prime
Minister's initial refusal to authorize an investigation. The turn-
about occurred only after the unprecedented, massive public outpouring.
And so, the more important lesson that we can derive from that set of

circumstances is that individual citizens have a role, perhaps the most important role, in holding their nation to elevated national standards. The individual citizen who holds no position of power at all can by either his silence or his protest finally make the real difference and that's a lesson we can all learn.

We derive another kind of instruction when we examine into the initial reaction of many Israeli and American Jewish leaders. Those reactions ranged from Prime Minister Begin's total disclaimer of responsibility which I have already mentioned, to reactions like my own, which were more common, I think, that Israel, having announced after the assassination of President-elect Gamayal that it was entering Beirut to maintain order there, had obviously failed in carrying out that responsibility, a responsibility which it did not have to assume but did, in fact, assume. What I am saying is that there was a range of views but the range was narrow. There was an almost universal assumption among Jews--the Israeli press was a notable exception--that Israel's responsibility was--at most--a responsibility for serious mistakes in judgment in allowing the so-called Christians into the camps in the first place and in waiting too long to stop the massacre once it was in progress. There was an almost universal assumption among Jews that the Israeli military command did not have--could not have had--an intention to cause a massacre or to permit a massacre of innocent Palestinians. I think that is true. We will not know until the investigation has been completed. There is something touching in that almost universal Jewish judgment. It is something like a mother's reaction when she learns that her son has been charged with a serious crime--"My son is not capable of such a thing." Such a reaction is understandable in parents. It is less excusable in the case of a whole people. It is in fact very, very dangerous. It is based, after all, on nothing more than a belief that Jews could not do a thing like that; that Jews are somehow immune from the more savage forms of human behavior; that Jews at least since some of the more gory episodes of 3,000 years ago set forth in the Holy Scriptures simply have been incapable of such acts, and that in light of the Holocaust it is obscene to accuse Jews of intending a massacre. I suggest to you that that is a dangerous view, which takes the most important lesson of the Holocaust and turns it on its head.

That lesson is a new awareness that _every_ human being carries within him the potential not only for glory, but for bestiality. That is the way we were made. We were made also with the ability to choose. If the Holocaust has not taught us that we must work hard to choose the good and to help each other choose the good, it has taught us very little. Through prayer, through education, through our awareness of history and the devestation that can be wrought by making the wrong choice, through an active conscience, through understanding the sin of silence, through an appreciation of those forms of government which tend to bring out the better qualities of their citizens--in all these ways, we must work to make certain that most humans choose the good. Let me repeat that I do not believe there was any Israeli intent that innocents be slaughtered. But an assumption that some of us are immune from such evil inclinations

is dangerous, self-evidently false, and a special form of arrogance
that ignores the most essential teaching of the Holocaust that we have
been trying to teach at these conferences for many years.

On other occasions, I have reviewed with audiences, mostly Jewish
audiences but not always, the 2,000 year trauma of the exiled Jews living in societies in which church and state were one. I always pointed
out that if Judaism had been the state religion in, say, 12th century
England, the persecutions might not have been very different--they
simply would have been happening to different people. It was the over-
concentration of power that was the root cause of the Jewish trauma. It
was not the church; it was not the state; it was the combination that
was deadly. For 2,000 years Jews in exile were powerless. There is a
downside and an upside of powerlessness. The downside of powerlessness is
that you become the victim. The upside, the benefit of powerlessness, is
that it instills empathy for others who are powerless. Now a new and
powerful Israeli nation has arisen out of the ashes of the Holocaust.
Will it use its new-found power to do good? I think it will. The
lessons to which the Jewish people have been exposed have had a saga-
like quality; it's almost mythical: 400 years as slaves in Egypt;
2,000 years in exile, and subject to the whims of the powerful; 6
million gassed and burned in ovens in our lifetimes. All have been
unbelievably painful lessons in the consequences of powerlessness. The
Jewish people have learned well one half of the lesson--that never again
must they be powerless in an unredeemed world. I believe they have
learned as well the other half of the lesson--that those who are powerless must never be abused by the Jewish people.

Which takes me to my final comments, concerning the Palestinian
Arabs. When two peoples have claim to the same land, either the two
peoples must be merged into one or the land must be divided in two.
That was self-evident when the United Nations voted to divide the remainder of Palestine in 1947. There was no Palestinian nationalism in
1947, however, and so Jordan, on its way to attacking Israel, simply
occupied the West Bank, annexed it and remained there for 19 years, until
the Six Day War in 1967. I have no recollection and neither do you of
a Palestinian National Movement working to throw off the yoke of their
Jordanian masters during those 19 years.

There was no sense of Palestinian nationhood in 1947, but there is
today, and those who say otherwise are blind to reality. But Palestinian
nationalism is very different from the nationalism of others. It was
born in hate, a hate purposely created and kept alive by Arab states
which manipulated Palestinian refugees and, despite their own vast resources, refused to resettle them for 35 years. For 35 years, Palestinian
Arabs have been taught to hate Israelis and their refugee camps have become the breeding ground for terrorism directed at Israel. It is not
the West Bank they have been taught to covet. I was arrested and jailed
in 1964 for demonstrating at the Jordanian pavilion at the New York
World's Fair which was being used to advertise the plight of Palestinian
refugees. It was not the West Bank the propoganda was aimed at. Jordan,

itself governed the West Bank in 1964. It was not the West Bank Palestinians were taught to covet; it was Israel

Oscar Hammerstein was right when he wrote that you have to be taught
to hate and fear, you have to be taught from year to year. And the
Palestinians have been taught to hate from year to year, for 35 years.
Palestinian nationalism is flawed by hate. And year by year, unfortunately, the Israelis have learned something too--distrust--increasing
distrust.

With all of that, the basic fact remains unchanged from 1947: When
two peoples lay claim to the same land either the two peoples must merge
into one or the land must be divided in two. But 35 years of Palestinian
hate and increasing Israeli distrust make that far more difficult today
than when it was supposed to have occurred in 1947 and it was far from
easy then. An outside observer might look today at the relative power
of the Israelis and powerlessness of the Palestinian Arabs and conclude
that magnanimity must come from the Israelis. That conclusion would be
wrong. The terrorist attacks on Israeli civilians over the past 35
years were conducted by these powerless people; and these powerless
people insist that their spokesman be an organization which to this day
asserts that when they have succeeded in liberating the West Bank, that
will be only the first stage toward their liberation of all of Palestine,
meaning Israel itself. Is it any wonder then that Israelis look upon an
independent Palestinian entity on the West Bank with the greatest fear
and trepidation?

When it is hate that spawns distrust, reconciliation can come about
only by dealing first with the hate. President Sadat understood that
well, and the world saw how quickly Israeli distrust dissolved once
Egyptian hatred dissolved. And so it is clear, to me at least, that
while Israel may be strong and the Palestinian Arabs weak, there will
be no reconciliation unless the Palestinian Arabs and the Arab states
which for 35 years have methodically instilled in them a pathological
hatred of Israel, come to understand that it is this hatred which is at
the root of their plight, and find a way to deal with it.

FROM GENERATION TO GENERATION

DR. MICHAEL FEUER

At the eighth annual Conference on the Holocaust the theme
is "Signs of Oppression" and participants seek lessons. We listen
to keynote addresses and panel discussions, eager to learn. Will
someone help us make sense of the concentration camps? The event
is organized mainly to give educators more material for their classrooms. But many come with a personal as well as a professional
mission: to reason things out is reassuring. Most of us probably
treat everyday problems with more humility; but we meet here to
take on the challenge of understanding Hitler's genocide, defiantly,
with a fist-waving faith in reason as the ultimate victor. I recall
my father telling me of roll-calls at Buchenwald, some of which he
endured by playing mental chess with a buddy or by listening to
lectures on psychoanalysis from one of Freud's former pupils. We
confront irrationality and barbarism with reason and civility.

I develop this theme during a panel session called "From Generation to Generation." My co-panelist is Yaffa Eliach, a scholar and
poet of the Holocaust who warns us that it is becoming a "non-Jewish
event" because most historical documents are German and most survivors
are dying before their stories are told. She is right; and who, if
not we,of the second generation, are closest to the personal histories?
But our ability to record the truth is fragile precisely because of our
unique access to the data. Can we listen, record, and re-tell our
parents' anguish? Can we survive, emotionally, without generalizations that diffuse the pain? Can we resist the temptation to impose
a logic that may not be there?

I tell of a highly respected Jewish historian who, addressing a
group of children of survivors, sympathized with our "trauma" (TIME
magazine had reported that the "trauma is passed on..."), and excused
our over-consumption of expensive clothing on the grounds of our
parents' suffering. What can we make of a claim whose premise is
casual (are there data on clothing purchases of survivors' children?)
and whose conclusion has no basis in scientific method? Coming from
one whose devotion to the Jewish community is well known, this is
nonsense without malice. By waiving the demands of rigorous scholar-
ship--her reputation is otherwise impeccable--she is perhaps reveal-
ing a deep need to endow the Holocaust with something that sounds
remotely logical. A familiar motif--penniless immigrants, opulent
children--makes her story at once respectful and reassuring: not
all human aspirations were destroyed by the Nazis. And more, the
possibility that expensive clothes might relieve psychic trauma gives
hope for how we and our children might survive the next one.

My lesson is that we who are so close to the history must find
the courage to reject the dishonest, albeit more comforting, versions.

The idea that survivor families ease their pain with designer jeans is consoling, as are other myths of "typical" survivor behavior; or of how those who really wanted to survive could; or of how the inmates liberated themselves. If children of survivors are really no more or less neurotic than the general population, is the grandeur, the sanctity, the uniqueness of the Holocaust in any way diminished? A prominent Philadelphia psychiatrist I know is apparently not willing to take the chance, and develops his research hypotheses on the premise that "the greatest catastrophe of Jewish history must have had effects on the families of survivors." I close with a plea for restraint. Glorifications, innocent fabrications, believable cause-effect scenarios, and analogies with other events are a crutch.

When our session ends, a woman who had hoped to read a prepared condemnation of our moderator (Ed Guthman of the PHILADELPHIA INQUIRER) for his newspaper's coverage of the war in Lebanon, asks me how I feel about the way she was called out of order. Before I can answer she illustrates the point of my lesson: "The way they shut me up, it was just like Nazi Germany." I look around the Holiday Inn for barbed wire and guns.

But why blame her? After all, Beirut reminded Pat Oliphant of the Warsaw Ghetto; Nicholas von Hoffman saw Israel "pounding the Star of David into a swastika"; and Menachem Begin pardons Israeli excesses with self-righteous lectures on Jewish martyrology as though his world view alone follows from the Holocaust. With those models, it is not surprising to hear a concerned Jew fall for the same silly analogies; the irony, of course, is that she had come to the Conference to attack the INQUIRER'S!

At least this one angry woman recognizes the irony and rewords her complaint. But the INQUIRER, whose influence is somewhat greater, has yet to disclaim Tony Auth's cartoons depicting Moses with horns and equating Auschwitz with Sidon; and Edward Herman's op-ed piece announcing that Arafat's good name has been smeared by an international Jewish conspiracy in much the same way the Jews of Europe had been maligned by the Nazis; and Richard Ben Kramer's front page dispatches from a Lebanese hospital that conveniently omitted the bit about a missile installation across the street. This suspension of journalistic ethics, in the INQUIRER as in much of the world press, may also reflect a need to assign simple logic to complex or painful events. But we expect more from our best editors; they may be simple but they are rarely pornographic. Worse yet, they now extend their irreverence to the Constitution, and defend their poor judgment with pompous cries of "free press," as though the first amendment prohibited integrity.

A few years before his death, I began pestering my father to record his memories, and I remember his reluctance. He had begun to doubt his capacity to remember accurately. And he had already seen others' accounts polished for Madison Avenue and Hollywood;

he had read his favorite reporters casually refer to "genocide" in Vietnam; he had learned that Auschwitz was now a popular device to spice up paperback cop thrillers; he had heard psychiatrists talk of "survivor syndrome" and later of "child-of-survivor syndrome"; he had observed the U.N. equating Zionism and Nazism.

I used to think hearing stories of the Holocaust was difficult; the real challenge is telling them.

DR. MEL MERMELSTEIN

I really appreciate your invitation. I would have come 10,000
miles to give you, particularly because you are teachers and educators,
a first-hand report about how I got involved in this lawsuit and what
this is all about. Why me? Why me of all the other survivors? Why
have they picked me, Mel Mermelstein, of all the other survivors to
come forth and prove that "Jews were gassed to death at Auschwitz."

After all, there were other survivors—there's Wiesenthal, there's
Elie Wiesel. I often wondered why they have not brought such lawsuits
against these so-called revisionists? I think I should leave that
question up to you. Perhaps we can deal with it during the questions
and answers.

Let me give you a brief up-date on how I got involved in this lawsuit.

Two years ago, to be exact, I received a phone call from a professor;
everything, somewhere along the line, begins with professors or universities.

In my case, too, it began with a professor who called me. I used
to speak at a class that he gives on the Holocaust, three times a year,
at the California State University, Long Beach. When he called, he
asked, "Mel, where are you? Why aren't you doing something? Haven't
you heard"? I said, "I don't know what you are talking about; be specific. You know I am ready and willing to help." He said, "No, that's
not it. We have a professor by the name of Buchner, who not only teaches
them that the Holocaust is a hoax, but takes students to his home and
teaches them that the Holocaust is a big lie: a Zionist plot." I said,
"Well, I'll tell you frankly—I've heard that before," and I further said
that I remembered back in 1977 when Elie Wiesel was a professor and a survivor of Auschwitz-Birkenau, just like I am, I heard him say it. By the
way, since then, I was able to uncover an A.D.L. Bulletin dated November,
1977, in which the very words which I heard Elie talked, screamed and
cried about are recorded here in this anti-defamation bulletin. It said
the following:

"I received a postcard addressed to me at Boston University.
It said, 'I recently completed reading a book, THE HOAX OF
THE 20TH CENTURY, copyright 1977. The professor who wrote
the postcard said that the 6,000,000 is total fiction. That
Jews were not gassed and put in the ovens in concentration
camps. There was nothing in their records to substantiate
the Jewish claims nor the confessions that were obtained
under duress. Then Elie cried and said, 'I guess Hitler was
right when he said the Jew was the master of the big lie.'
I received a letter from a professor at Sorbonne: 'Yes, there
were ovens, but only for the sick people; never were there any
gas chambers.'"

"There is a movement now, not only to rewrite history,
but to destroy it. In so doing, humble and humiliate
those teachers who still not only remember, but <u>Are Here</u>."

Then he goes on again:

"If we are to believe those morally deranged, perverted,
so-called historians, that the victims did not perish,
then six million Jews blackmailed the German people."

This is what Elie said five years ago; he received a postcard
and a letter, too.

I am not here to criticize Elie, I'm here to feel for him, it was
so painful for Elie; I remember, I remember his expression.

So, this is what I told my friend, the professor from Cal State.
"I heard that before; what do you want me to do"? He answered, "Oh,
I don't know; let's do something. Let's call a press conference."
"A news conference, then what? All you are going to do is give them
more publicity," I said. "No, it has to be exposed; it has to be
dealt with." "Why don't we just call the Simon Wiesenthal Center.
That is all we had."

"What is there to do," I said. "No one would listen. No one
wants to cooperate."

I went home. I was angry. I like to write letters, so I did. I
wrote letters to the editor in which I brought out as to who this so-
called revisionist group really is. I wrote a letter to the editor
and asked my secretary to send it out to at least a half dozen or so
newspapers to see if they would give it a tumble; sure enough they did.
Within a few days, two newspapers locally published my letter; then,
THE JERUSALEM POST, International Edition, published it, as well. I
don't want to spend too much time on this because I know you want to
ask questions. However, the letter stated as follows:

First, I asked the reader whether or not they had heard of these
so-called prestigious gentlemen's organization known as the Institute
of Historical Review. Perhaps, if they had not, allow me to tell you
about them:

> Bennett - a member of the Civil Liberties of Australia
> Dr. Reinhart Buchner - Cal State, Long Beach
> Dr. Arthur Butz - Northwestern University
> Dr. Robert Foreson - University of Lyon, France
> Dietrich Felderer - Bible Researcher - Sweden. I wanted to
emphasize that because he became a defendant in my lawsuit. Last
September, I discovered that he was going to be in Chicago from
Stockholm so, we served him with papers.

Well, I went on further:

If by chance you have not heard about these gentlemen nor read about the journal of the so-called Historical Review, allow me to inform you that these university professors, some of them former Nazis of the old Hitlerite Regime, these former Nazis have taken upon themselves to use and abuse our colleges and universities, particularly in the United States to spread lies, hatred and bigotry about the subject known as the Holocaust.

They even invented new titles to distort the event, "The Myth of the Six Million," "The Hoax of the 20th Century." What can I say? Once again these highly acclaimed professors of highly accredited universities are at it again. They are teaching our new generation that the chimneys at Auschwitz were bakeries.

This letter went on and on and I don't want to go on any further except to say that shortly after the letter appeared in THE JERUSALEM POST, a response came from no other than Dietlieb Felderer and this is what he wrote to THE JERUSALEM POST:

I have received some rather discourteous news which includes most vile accusations. The problem seems to originate with a letter from Melvin Mermelstein, which apparently is covered in your paper of August 17, which included the writer and a list of personalities, actively denying the Holocaust. I am hoping to be able to reassure him and, if possible, see him at Auschwitz in October where we can discuss the problem. The letter has caused me a great deal of suffering. I had nothing to do with Nazism; in fact, I have not been politically involved in my whole life. I was born in 1942 in the midst of the Nazi turmoil and our family suffered a lot during the war. Furthermore, my relations with the synagogue here in Sweden are good. Furthermore, my relations with the Jews here are of the best and I have participated in services although not being a regular memeber. It is a cordial relationship between us and I hope to reassure my many friends in Israel and elsewhere, who otherwise might get a distorted view of my good intentions. Signed, Dietlieb Felderer.

Underneath that was another letter from an un-named lady who said:

I recently arrived here (in Israel) from Sweden, as a new immigrant. I was appalled to see in print the letter from Mr. Felderer, from Stockholm, in an issue of my daily paper, THE JERUSALEM POST. This Mr. Felderer is known as one of the biggest antisemites in Sweden. Some years ago, he opened an office called, "Jewish Information" at his private address outside of Stockholm. Of the many activities in this office, he produced about 30 or 40 leaflets denying that the Jews were being exterminated in World War II. He has tried to propogate similar ideas among school youth. He has translated German books of an extremely antisemitic nature. He has also harrassed several prominent Jews. Mr. Felderer claims he is a good friend of the Jews in Stockholm. To the best of my knowledge, he does not have a single Jewish friend in Stockholm and, in fact, the community has on several occasions tried to take him to court. In order to avoid unpleasantness to the families in Sweden, I omit my family name.

Here is one more letter, because the letter comes from Mr. Levi, the executive director of the Jewish community in Stockholm, and responds to Felderer's letter:

On October 14, you carried a letter from Felderer, in Stockholm, reporting a letter from Mr. Mermelstein of August 17, which listed Felderer as one of the persons denying the Holocaust. To put the record straight, we would like to point out that Felderer is, indeed, running a campaign in Sweden, through his obscure organization, "Bible Researcher," denying the fact of the Holocaust. He is spreading leaflets in Swedish in Swedish schools, inciting students to ask teachers the "truth" of the Holocaust, offering huge sums to persons and youths who can prove they saw gas chambers, and denying Nazi atrocities, as well. Felderer has no relationship with any synagogue in Stockholm. Furthermore, he has no good intentions in this matter. I urge readers not to believe or trust him.

Right after that, I received a letter. They couldn't stand my letter to the Editors. Apparently, that letter I received on the 20th of November, 1980, was signed by the so-called Institute for Historical Review, Director, Lewis Brandon. By the way, this letter was delivered by U. S. mail to my office in California.

Your recent letter in THE JERUSALEM POST, indicates that you can prove that Jews were gassed to death at Auschwitz.

At our 1979 Revisionists convention, we announced a $50,000 reward for proof of this allegation. To date, no one has stepped forward and at the 1980 Revisionists convention, we suspended that reward. However, we replaced it with a $25,000 reward to prove that the diary of Anne Frank is authentic; another $25,000 reward to prove Jews were turned into bars of soap by the Nazis.

A letter like that to a survivor? Then they go on further to tell me that under the circumstances, they will reinstate the $50,000 reward so that I can apply. Then it says that they enclosed forms for me and that the evidence will be judged along the same standards as evidence in a United States criminal court, not the standards of the Nuremberg trials.

Then it goes on further to say that if we do not hear from you, we will be obliged to draw our own conclusions and publicize this fact to the mass media. In other words, they are going to expose me to the mass as a liar.

Now, I would like to be able to put the shoe on the other foot. Suppose you got a letter like that, read it and are a survivor of the Holocaust. Not only that, but in 1944, I will give you the exact date, May 22, I saw with my own eyes, my own mother and my two sisters among others, how they were lured and driven into the gas chambers--#5 at Birkenau.

After reading that letter, I decided to consult with a Jewish organization I have supported for years. They refused my plea for help. After all, I was supporting Jewish institutions for years. As a matter of fact, to this day, I am on the board of some of them. I took that letter and discussed it with their legal counsel at the regional office and I said, "Read this letter." He read it and said, "It's signed by a non-existent non-person." "What are you talking about"? I asked what to do about it. How much do you know? What do you know about the organization? I got no response. I felt beat. I really did. I felt almost as I did when I went back home after I was liberated from Buchenwald. I didn't know too much about my brother. I did know that I had no father. I suspected something wrong with my mother and two sisters because from time to time we would be able to hear through friends or someone from another camp that "I saw your sisters. My mother was only 44. She was a seamstress, so I had hopes that someday--a little bit of hope left in me. When I got home in 1945, in July, and it was revealed to me that I had no one, that's exactly how I felt when I was urged to "forget it." I was beaten.

I began to talk to my wife about it and luckily I do have a family that is very understanding and I was told to do whatever I had to do. I said, "Yes, I need a lawyer. I am not going to give in to these scums, and I am not going to dignify them with a response. I want legal action. I will not respond to that letter." My wife said, "Why don't you give Bill Cox a call"? He had read my book about a year and a half ago or so and was very affected by it. So, I did. I told him about the letter. He said to come over and we'll talk about it. We sat down and he read the letter and he said, "You know, I can tell you, the letter by itself is not actionable." Again I felt beaten. I said, "Bill, isn't there some way you can make it actionable"? Well, he went through different ways and methods and whatever. He was as disturbed as I was about the letter. We let it go for a few days and decided to meet later in the week.

I phoned my lawyer and we decided to go over the letter and the whole issue again. "I think there is hope," Bill said. We sat down and he gave me a brief description of what he was able to learn about this venomous group. We can apply an old law. They sent you a letter offering you a $50,000 reward to prove something and he gave me an example. In the old days, communication was no where near what it is today and if someone had written you a letter from New York offering you a parcel of land for $1,000 and you accepted, that was a binding contract. We will do the same thing with these "bastards." We'll send them a letter and say, I accept the offer of $50,000 and I will be able to prove that Jews were gassed to death at Auschwitz because I was in Auschwitz, having seen my mother and two sisters who were led and driven with others into what I discovered to be gas chambers. I will be a good and legitimate witness. According to California code, I am a good witness having seen Jews gassed to death in Auschwitz. I am not the only one, by the way. However, in this particular case, my lawyer explained to me, I am a good witness.

So, we did that. However, the acceptance that we were ready and willing to prove that Jews were gassed to death in Auschwitz was also predicated on, unless they respond in 30 days, we will take them to court. Well, 30 days went by and we hadn't heard from them. It was exactly as my attorney had predicted. He shot them another letter to say "waht gives"? Then, they came back and said, "We just got another letter from Simon Wiesenthal. We decided to take Simon Wiesenthal before we could take you.

My attorney went to Superior Court and filed a lawsuit against them for breach of contract, etc.

Since then, we began our discovery proceedings. We are talking about a year and a half to two years—depositions to try to get a hold of this Lewis Brandon. He was not available. My attorney went to court and asked the judge for a motion to produce this witness. The judge ordered and he came. We got his deposition. We got Mrs. Carto's deposition and, by the way, Mrs. Carto is the wife of the head of the Liberty Lobby. She is a German national, carries a German passport. She was deposed for five hours and then the director was deposed for five hours by their attorney. We had been to court about a half dozen times and finally, on October 9, 1981, the judge of the Superior Court declared the following because we went in for summary judgment. He convinced the opposition that they also submit the summary judgment without waiting for a long, dragged out date for a trial. The judge declared the following, that "This Court takes judicial notice of the fact that Jews were gassed to death in Auschwitz concentration camp in Poland and that the Holocaust is not reasonably subject to dispute and it is capable of immediate and accurate determination by resort to sources of reasonably indisputable accuracy"and before he dropped his gavel, he said, "It is simply a fact," which proves them to be liars.

Since then, we served the Washington-based Liberty Lobby, and filed for a trial date which will last about 30 days. There are five causes of action which call for punitive and other damages against the defendants, amounting to $17,000,000 plus $50,000.

JUDAISM AND THE JEWISH PEOPLE

new and forthcoming from

THE EDWIN MELLEN PRESS

The Image of the Non-Jew in Judaism: An Historical and Constructive Study of the Noahide Laws, David Novak (Congregation Darchay Noam)

Lily Montagu and the Advancement of Liberal Judaism: From Vision to Vocation, Ellen Umansky (Emory University)

Mordecai M. Kaplan and the Development of Reconstructionism, Richard Libowitz (Carleton College)

Louis Meyer's Eminent Hebrew Christians of the Nineteenth Century, edited by David Rausch (Ashland College)

A New Jewish Ethics, S. Daniel Breslauer (University of Kansas)

Identity Maintenance and Accommodation to Modernity In Orthodox Judaism, Charles Selengut (Morris County C. C.)

Author as Character in the Writings of Sholem Aleichem, Victoria Aarons (Trinity University)

Human Responses to the Holocaust: Perpetrators and Victims, Bystanders and Resisters, edited by Michael Ryan (Drew University)

EUCHARISTIA in Philo, Jean LaPorte (Notre Dame University)

HUMAN RESPONSES TO THE HOLOCAUST: PERPETRATORS AND VICTIMS, BYSTANDERS AND RESISTERS,

edited by

Michael Ryan.

Reviews

From the
Journal of
Ecumenical Studies

The Scholars' Conference on the Church Struggle and the Holocaust met annually at Temple University from 1970 to 1975, when the National Conference of Christians and Jews took over the planning and organization of the conferences. The papers from the 1979 Conference are on the subjects mentioned in the title, and more.

The section on perpetrators and victims includes an analysis of Hitler which explains why he specifically designed the murder of European Jewry (The Author is quite properly embarrassed for documenting the obvious in order to refute pseudo-scholarly baloney.); the first history of the development of the concentration camp as an institution, along with brief case studies of the staffs of the various types of camps; some unfortunately poorly reproduced photographs of Bergen-Belsen by a member of the British liberation forces; and an eerie, understated account of a victim called upon to identify his persecutors.

The section on bystanders and resisters analyzes the powerlessness of the Jewish establishment in the United States to act on behalf of the victims; the rescue of Danis Jewry as a catalyst for the movement from passive to active resistance in occupied Denmark; the disorganized, and yet successful, resistance of the churches in occupied Holland; the heroic Christian witness of Helmuth James von Moltke; and the youthful agonizing of Adam von Trott, who took a job in the Nazi foreign service in order to resist from within.

The first of the additional sections is "Post-Holocaust Theological and Ethical Reflections." It contains essays— one by a Christian and one by a Jew—on the convergence and divergence of Christian and Jewish messianism after the Holocaust. There is also a provocative article on "biomedical issues" (i.e., killing by doctors) in our society which challenges the reader to distinguish between the "quality of life" argument for euthanasia and abortion today from Nazi extermination propaganda.

A bibliography of the Holocaust from periodicals from 1950 to the present rounds out the volume.

The book has several noteworthy features. Foremost is that, for a book on the Holocaust, this volume is surprisingly not gloomy. The atrocities are not adumbrated, except as they are stirred up within the imaginzation of the reader (making them truly horrifying for those who know the details from elsewhere). The book provokes the reader to assess what his or her own position would be with respect to the Holocaust and congeners in our own days. More than one of the Christians in the book express admiration for the dignity with which the Jews met their fate. How welcome a change this attitude is from the "sheep-led-to-the-slaughter" image prevalent in some quarters!

Although there are exceptions, there is in general a puzzling lack of assessment of guilt to anyone but the Nazis—and that only to the Nazi leaders. I found it disturbing that even the thoughtful Moltka is not portrayed as aware that Nazi Antisemitism did not spring full-grown from nowhere, but was nurtured in a cultural medium.

Those interested in ecumenical relations will find the latter two-thirds of the book to contain valuable case histories of ecumenism in action (and inaction), on the part of both individuals and institutions. Unfortunately, the articles on messianism, which explicitly invite dialogue, are not substantial enough.

Anyone who has seen the relatively sparce grove at Yad Vashem in Jerusalem, which is dedicated to the memory of Gentiles who aided Jews, is certain to welcome the accounts in this book of the efforts by Christians and their churches on behalf of Jews.

The book as a whole is certainly to be recommended.

R. David Freedman
University of California, Davis, CA

From
Choice

HUMAN RESPONSES TO THE HOLOCAUST: perpetrators an victims, bystanders and resisters, ed. by Michael D. Ryan.

The destruction of European Jewry is the central focus of this series of papers presented at a meeting of scholars in 1979, sponsored by the National Conference of Christians and Jews. Although all of the papers can be understood by the layman or nonscholar, the essays address themselves to particular issues rather than to general aspects of the Holocaust. The common theme of many essays is the ethical problem of the human response to the horror. Thus, for example, there is an evaluation of the effectiveness of the response of the American Jewish community to the events of the war years, another on the resistance of the Church in Holland, and one dealing with the career of an unusual German highly placed in the Army who clearly opposed Nazism. There are also several essays that deal with the theological implications of the Holocaust for both Christians and Jews. This volume contains an extensive bibliography of articles that have appeared in the general press between 1960 and 1968.

SYMPOSIUM SERIES